Brief Welcome Speeches

Amy Bolding

BAKER BOOK HOUSE

Grand Rapids, Michigan 49506

Formerly published under the title:
New Welcome Speeches

Sixth printing, October 1988

ISBN: 0-8010-0856-5

PHOTOLITHOPRINTED BY CUSHING - MALLOY, INC.
ANN ARBOR, MICHIGAN, UNITED STATES OF AMERICA

Contents

Words of Welcome

... For Visitors

We are happy to have among our visitors today a group from _____ College. These young people will be our leaders of tomorrow. As they sing and give their testimonies we hope you will receive a blessing.

★   ★   ★

Among our many visitors this special Sunday we have Mr. and Mrs. _____, parents of our pastor. They are always welcome in our services. We love them because they have given us their son; at least they share him with us. We keep him so busy his parents have to visit to get a glimpse of him.

★   ★   ★

This is our Homecoming Day. We are gratified at the large number of visitors. Some have traveled quite a distance to be able to spend this day with us. Greet everyone you meet and make them feel welcome. You will find name tags in the foyer. Wearing a tag will keep from embarrassment at forgotten names. Visitors, we are glad you are here. We want your homecoming to be happy and give you a spiritual blessing. Your coming has already helped to make the day a pleasant one.

★   ★   ★

Will all the guests in our audience please stand? Now will all the homefolk take note of our guests and be sure to greet them at the close of the service.

★   ★   ★

We welcome Rev. _____. He comes to us from a wonderful church. He has been highly recommended by one we all know well: Mr. _____, who has worked with him before. Weeks of preparation have gone into planning and getting ready for Rev. _____'s visit. Now the time has arrived and he is here. Let us make this an outreach time. May there be many testimonies of success in soul-winning when this week is over.

★   ★   ★

There is a sound of much going on in our camp. We are counting it a real blessing to have so many young people filling our auditorium for each session. It is an unforgettable experience to meet fine Christian youth on the paths of our campground. We are truly seeing a demonstration for Chirst by our youth.

★   ★   ★

Mr. _____ has come to our church to lead us in reaching for a record. We have been going along in an ordinary way but now we must shift into high gear. We want to reach for a record, and Mr. _____ knows just how to lead us in this. Every person with a place of responsibility in our church must cooperate in this effort to reach a record. We are counting on you!

★   ★   ★

We are glad to have Mr. _____ in our audience today. He is a member of the Board of Trustees for _____. He is one man we feel tries to stand for the right.

★   ★   ★

Sports have always had a place in the American life. Yet there has never been a time in our history when sports were more popular than now. We admire a winner. We listen to his accomplishments and some try to follow his instructions.

We welcome here today a man who is a good sportsman. We are sincere in our congratulations. He has reached the top by hard training and concentration.

★   ★   ★

Someone has said: "The right path is straight and narrow — and all uphill."

We welcome one who has known much climbing uphill. He has climbed to the top in spite of many setbacks in health. He is here at our invitation to tell us how faith, hope, and love will see a man through.

★ ★ ★

The youth in each generation wants to do their thing. Most of us remember other ways of expressing our desires for recognition. We welcome one tonight who is still young, who chose for his special thing to do, a task not easy to accomplish. He is a great musician and has promised me we will have a variety of numbers for all ages.

★ ★ ★

We wish to say "Welcome" to the stars and super stars of our football team. We are proud to honor them with this banquet. They honored us by the way they played and won the games this season.

★ ★ ★

Holidays are happy days for us. We are so glad to welcome so many students home for the vacation. We want you to find your places of service in our church during these holidays. Perhaps many of you will have time to drop by the church office and visit in a more personal way.

★ ★ ★

We are glad to welcome a new family in our services. Mr. and Mrs. _____ and children. Will you please stand. He is to be our new Educational Director. This place on our staff has been vacant some time. We sought the leadership of God in finding just the right man for the task.

I know you will welcome this family and help them get settled in a new place, new schools, and new friends.

★ ★ ★

We will enjoy hearing our new Music Director sing today.

9

We feel he has left a field where he was greatly beloved to come and serve among us. He worked for _____ a number of years. Someone said the last services he attended there seemed more like funeral services. People were sad at his leaving. We must in no way make him sorry he came to us.

★ ★ ★

Brother _____, pastor at _____ is on vacation and chose to worship with us today. We are glad you came our way. We hear many good things about your fine ministry in _____. Welcome!

★ ★ ★

We are honored today to have Boy Scout Troop _____ as our special guests. God has given us an opportunity to minister to these fine boys. Their counselor is a member of our church and they meet in one of the Sunday School rooms.

We are proud of you boys and hope you will learn much more than just outdoor activities this year.

★ ★ ★

On this beautiful Easter Sunday we are pleased to welcome many visitors. We hope you will feel the gladness of the Easter season. We want you to have the peace of God's promises in your hearts. May you be filled with the spirit of love as you worship with us today.

★ ★ ★

We welcome the football team of _____ School in our services today. We consider you someone special to know. We have watched you play and whether you win or lose we are always proud of your fine spirit of sportsmanship.

★ ★ ★

In this huge crowd today we hope to witness an outpouring of God's spirit. We know our many guests will enter into the spirit of the services and pray with us for the outpouring of God's love.

. . . For School Officials

We of the _____ faculty, staff and student body cordially welcome you to our campus.

We are proud of the overall educational process carried on in our school.

We are honored that you took time on this occasion to visit this institution. Please make yourself acquainted with its facilities. Please come often to visit us and encourage others to do the same.

★   ★   ★

We are happy to welcome Dr. _____ as our guest. His administration at _____ has been marked by a rejuvenation of high ideals, better methods, and new procedures. He will bring a breath of growth and accomplishment to our campus.

★   ★   ★

We are honored to have as our speaker Dr. _____. He is a man with a multipurpose education. He has degrees from several colleges. He is adept at using his special talents to encourage young people and help them find their own special talents.

★   ★   ★

After meeting our speaker I had the feeling that he is a God-ordained link in the chain of life, especially forged and divinely called to lead youth to a better life. He comes to us with fresh ideas and plans for a greater school.

★   ★   ★

Have you ever asked yourself, Could I have witnessed more diligently? Mr. _____ is a man who asked that question and then went out to do something about answering the question.

He is dedicated to making an impact for Jesus Christ

wherever he goes. You will find _____ to be one of the most unusual and interesting men you have ever met.

★ ★ ★

In the _____ years Dr. _____ has lived in our city he has carved a niche for himself on campus and in community activities off campus.

He makes his interest in students felt both on and off campus.

★ ★ ★

Mr. _____ is one of the most sports-minded men in our city. Yet he counts the day lost when he has not in some way witnessed for Christ. He likes to back a winning team. The greatest team of all, in his opinion, is the team of Christian students working to make the world a better place.

★ ★ ★

Here is a man with a positive attitude and an optimistic view toward the future. Wherever he goes he is a winner. It is a pleasant experience to be able to introduce to you a man of so many talents and such a variety of experiences.

It gives us a great deal of pride to see a man who can so ably communicate his Christian ideals to those on campus.

★ ★ ★

Welcome aboard, _____, we are thrilled to have you on our staff.

★ ★ ★

We have extended a unanimous call to Mr. _____ to be our Youth Director. We are glad to have him present for his first service with us. He was born in _____. His parents are Mr. and Mrs. _____ of that city.

He has been active in campus activities in _____ College. He will lead our youth in every area of our church program. His coming is an answer to prayer. I hope all will cooperate fully with his program and plans.

★ ★ ★

Praise God from whom all blessings flow! God has been especially good to us in sending Mr. _____ to work as our Minister of Education. He has won some great victories in the church, from which he comes. I felt God's presence strongly as our committee talked with him and offered him the place on our staff. Now he is here ready to start work with a bang.

He will be trying to involve as many in the working program of our church as possible. Plan to be a worker.

★　★　★

Mr. _____ is here on invitation from our church to look over our people and our plant. He is known as a young disciplinarian! That is what we need, at times. He also has the reputation of being a good organizer. We want to improve. I believe he can lead us in improvement

Introductions

... For Men (general)

In this day of change and unrest, we often ask ourselves: Is there a way to live in this materialistic age and still be a strong witness for Christ?

Our speaker today has found a way to answer this question. While many people today are engulfed in today's trend of materialism, Mr. _____, lets nothing interfere with his Christian witness. He spends time away from his business going from place to place giving his testimony.

We have looked forward to his visit and now we will hear him gladly.

★   ★   ★

Every talent we have is a God-given trust. He just trusted some with more than others. Our speaker is one with an over-abundance of blessing. He is sensitive to what is going on around him. At the same time he is uniquely different. He is a successful man, yet one deeply committed to Christ and His cause. Our speaker is a product of our times. He was born with talent and he has developed that talent. I am proud to introduce you to my friend, Mr. _____.

★   ★   ★

We have with us today a man who is a specialist in more fields than one. He is especially gifted in promoting the cause of Christ. He not only wants to tell us what has made his life different but what will give us new life.

Mr. _____ came up the hard way and landed on top. He used skill, perseverance and hard work to accomplish his success.

★   ★   ★

I want you to know a fine, intelligent man. He has been

my friend for a number of years. His messages are whole-some and enlightening.

★   ★   ★

Mr. _____ has not achieved his success by riding on the accomplishments of others. He is one man who faithfully fulfills his assignments. He even did his homework when he was a boy in school.

★   ★   ★

Teddy Roosevelt once said: The best executive is the one who has sense enough to pick good men to do what he wants done, and self-restraint enough to keep from meddling with them while they do it.

I want to introduce you to my boss, I think he is one of the best executives I know.

★   ★   ★

Since coming to _____ Mr. _____ has been a popular speaker for civic and church groups. He is the type of person who does things. He does not just think about some good advancements people might make, he finds no excuses for not doing something. He gets busy and does lots and lots of things.

★   ★   ★

Not too many years ago a man moved to our city. He has made himself known to the people in our community by his willingness to take part in civic affairs. He gives liberally of his time and money to help worthy causes. We feel fortunate indeed to have him speak to us and tell us more about his latest project.

★   ★   ★

Our special guest tonight is a music teacher. At times he feels he is inadequate to cope with the younger generation.

The other day he was trying to start off a new pupil. "Now Son what is a scale?" he asked after trying to point out things in the music book.

The new pupil, his mind far away on the bank of a creek replied, "I think it is a freckle on a fish."

★ ★ ★

I have heard Mr. _____ is a collector of rare items. I believe he has brought three of the most beautiful items in his collection with him tonight. Will the speaker's wife and two beautiful daughters please stand?

We are so glad you came along to make our evening more interesting.

★ ★ ★

Mr. _____ has not had any medals struck in his honor, but we certainly want to say we think he deserves a medal for coming tonight.

★ ★ ★

Our speaker is a man who has been worshipfully acclaimed by many people. I am sure he has also been criticized by hostile foes. Through all his popularity or non-popularity he has remained a person with great purpose and great personal charm.

★ ★ ★

Mr. _____ has put forth much effort in behalf of oppressed humanity. His kindness and good counseling record has been spread by word of mouth to the far corners of our state. He has made an ineradicable mark on the lives of many people.

★ ★ ★

Mr. _____ is a man of great courage. In the face of discouraging physical handicaps he has successfully attained many goals a lesser man would have considered unattainable.

★ ★ ★

It is my joy to present a man of importance in our city. He is a dynamic leader who has found victory through great sacrifice of time and money for a cause.

★ ★ ★

Mr. _____ is a man of faith, character, and progressive ideas. He is loved by many people for the magnanimity of his spirit. He is kind to those in trouble, sympathetic to those in need, firm with those who are wayward. He is what we might call "A character." God grant we may have more men of character like him.

★   ★   ★

With riots in the streets and on the campus, America needs to turn back to God. Mr. _____, spends much of his time going about, trying to arouse the people to an awakening. A religious awakening could turn our country back to God and change the downhill course we now seem to be following.

★   ★   ★

Mr. _____ is a popular television speaker so you may already feel you know him. We are honored that he could spare the time for this appearance in our meeting.

President Nixon once suggested we lower our voices so we can hear what each other is saying. Let us lower our voices and hear a great message from our guest speaker. Our speaker today is one who in place of spending his time in protest marches, sleep-ins, stand-ins, and sit-ins, went out and put on a work-in. He worked his way through college. He has worked in a successful job just as much as possible since college. In his spare time, which is very little, he has gone about trying to encourage people to make the most of the great opportunities our land offers.

★   ★   ★

In all of life there must be some who run the show and some who listen and observe. Mr. _____, is not the type to listen. He has observed, and today will tell us to what conclusions his observations have led him. He is certainly the type to plan and run the show. He has helped many people to find a new goal in life.

★   ★   ★

I asked Dr. _____'s son what his daddy did when he preached. "Oh, he huffs and he puffs until he blows the house down." Well, we are here tonight to hear a great minister. If he blows the house down maybe he will wake us up to our responsibilities as Christians.

★　★　★

Our speaker tonight is very nice looking, ladies, but he is married. He says he has been married _____ years and still can't afford it.

The girl who used to sink in his arms now has her arms in his sink.

★　★　★

I really don't know how to introduce this politician. He says his politics are mixed. He is a Republican, his father is a Democrat, his children are wet, the family cat is on the fence.

★　★　★

Once there happened to be a hog and a hen walking down the street. They saw a sign in a window; "Ham and eggs."

The hog said: "Now to you that is just a day's work but to me it is a real sacrifice."

Our speaker is one who counts just a day's work, not enough. He makes a real sacrifice in service. No day is too short for him to serve the Lord, no night too dark for him to fail to go when called.

★　★　★

Brother _____ was speaking to a civic club in Tulsa. In his opening prayer he prayed for the "pure and humble." A listener broke in and said; "Say a word for 'Gulf' also."

... For Teachers

A small boy brought home his report card. His father was disturbed at the grades, "Your teacher must think you are very stupid."

"Well daddy, no wonder he thinks I am stupid, I'm only in the fifth grade and he is a college graduate."

Our speaker has so many degrees from colleges he will probably think we are stupid. From the good reports we hear about Dr. _____, we expect to go home with our hearts inspired and our minds enriched.

★ ★ ★

Our speaker Dr. _____, is a graduate of _____ University. He is a great man doing a good work. Of course, not all people think so. The other night Dr. and Mrs. _____ were out for the evening and left a maid in charge. The phone rang and a voice frantically said, "I need a Doctor quick, is Dr. _____ at home?"

"He is not at home," the maid replied, "and besides if he were at home he is not the kind of a doctor that's good for doctoring."

We expect him to doctor our thinking, to prescribe the right solutions to our problems, and help us face today's problems with a better outlook and more courage.

★ ★ ★

Miss _____ is a teacher from _____. She tells me teaching our modern youth is not like walking along a garden path with only beauty and peace on either side. On the other hand she feels constantly challenged to try new ways, new paths to reaching bright minds.

She is well known in her school for her ability to cope with some serious problems of children. We hope tonight we catch a spark from her message to set us on fire to do more with the youth in our own city.

As a young man, Mr. _____, started on a journey. He planned on the journey being short and only a means to an end. The years have passed by and he is still on the same journey, the journey of teaching. His plans to quit and go into business as soon as he had saved some money, were forgotten. He saw in teaching a way to help humanity. We are proud of his accomplishments in our city, some of you present here sat in his classes or talked over problems with him. We are glad his journey as a teacher has kept him in our school system.

★   ★   ★

Professor _____ is a man who inspires zeal in his pupils. He creates in them a desire to learn more. If he discovers enthusiasm for a certain subject in a young person, he finds a way to help that pupil develop his abilities. I am proud to have such a man for a friend.

★   ★   ★

Any pupil reflects what he sees and hears. The pupils who have been under the influence of Professor _____, reflect his wholesome outlook on life.

His personal influence and teaching has resulted in a generation of brilliant scholars and business men coming from the _____ school.

He has helped bridge the years for many young people; between their first time away from home, and their complete dependence upon their abilities in a world of competition.

We are proud to have a man of Professor _____, capabilities and reputation to speak at this time.

★   ★   ★

A new boy from way up in the hills came to Professor _____'s school the other day. He was eager to learn and asked questions about everything he saw.

In the new school he saw some electricians at work.

"What are those men doing?" he asked Professor _____.

"They are putting in an electric switch."

The boy started up in alarm.

"I'm going back to the hills," he exclaimed. "I won't stay in a school where they do the switching by machinery."

We are glad to say not all of his pupils have gone away in fright. Many fine men and women have sat under the teaching of our speaker. We are eager to hear his views on our world today, and the place of youth in this world.

... For Public Officials

What Care I?
What care I who gets the credit?
Only let the work be done!
Christ himself will handle the credits
With the setting of the sun.
While the world is sick and waiting
For something I can be,
Help me Lord, in stress and struggle
Just to keep my eyes on Thee.

★ ★ ★

As a leader in our State politics, Mr. _____, has kept his eyes on high goals. He has strived to make his term in office contribute to the enrichment of the people, to the achievement of more abundant living for all. We feel civilization has been improved because he has served his people well.

Enthusiasm makes the difference in anything! Mr. _____ is enthusiastic about the task to which we have elected him.

We are glad to welcome him to share some of his zeal and enthusiasm with us today.

★ ★ ★

We have with us today a man well known by name if not in person to all of you. The Bible tells us, "A good name is rather to be chosen than great riches."

★ ★ ★

The motto of most politicians is; "It's a great life if you weaken a little."

I want to introduce to you a public official who tries never to weaken when the good of the community is at stake.

★ ★ ★

Senator _____ has invested his life in the important

affairs of public office. About all the majority of us know about public affairs is our own opinion and we plan to abide by it. We will hear how someone close to the law-making of our country arrives at his opinions. We may even have more sympathy for our office holders after we hear Senator _____ tell of some of his experiences.

★ ★ ★

Mr. _____ is a concerned politician. He is concerned over the crime situation in our state. He will tell us some of the things he has uncovered in his search for a way to make our state a better, safer place to live.

★ ★ ★

_____ took office last January. Since that time he has been a very busy man. He has met many important people and has been places most of us will never go, but I am glad to say he met many of us this evening with the same old smile and handshake that put him in office. We are proud to have him represent us.

★ ★ ★

Many politicians are slight-of-tongue artists.

★ ★ ★

This man has a good name in our community, county, and state. They say success is relative and individual and personal, yet I feel many of you have helped this man in his success by voting for him each election day.

We wish to congratulate him on the great job he is doing as he represents us in an important place.

★ ★ ★

Senator _____ has all kinds of experiences as he goes about trying to get votes. The other day he walked up to a man on the street corner. He gave the loafer a cigar and said: "Would you mind telling me your politics?"

"Why" was the reply, "I don't have any regular connections, but I sort of lean toward the Methodist."

We all have our own ideas about how we lean but we are looking forward to hearing our guest speak.

★　　★　　★

We are grateful for the record our speaker has for standing for the right. We have enjoyed his characteristic courtesy and jokes as we visited with him earlier. He has respect for his fellow man and will listen to the opinion of others.

Mr. _____ has given _____ years of service to the public. He has made some enemies and many friends. He will speak to us on a subject he feels fitting for our times and problems.

. . . For Evangelists

The evangelistic team of _____ and _____ will be with us this week. They are two great men. They are doing an outstanding work for God in their field. Please attend our services and pray for these two leaders.

★　★　★

We expect special blessings this week as we are led in evangelistic services by _____. Evangelists seem to live in paradise, going about eating fried chicken and having pie and cake every day. Would you like to be gone from home for weeks at a time? They really live a sacrificial life. Breathe a prayer for our Evangelist this week and back him with your presence.

★　★　★

Many victories will be won this week if you attend our revival services. Brother _____ is a man of God but he did not bring a revival in his pocket. We will have to visit, attend services, and pray, if we are going to have a great victory over sin.

★　★　★

If you have been experiencing something of the "generation gap," be sure to attend the youth revival. _____ will bring the messages. He is a graduate of one of our best colleges. He has had lots of experience working with youth while he was a student. Since graduation he has given full time to revivals.

★　★　★

They tell me that a man is young so long as he radiates hope for our future. Our visiting Evangelist is the most optimistic man I have ever met. Yet do not come to the services expecting to hear soft-spoken sermons about peace and hope. He is a minister who calls a spade a spade and sets to work to dig out evil and preach a better life way.

★　★　★

Our visiting minister is a Tall Texan with a Texas drawl but don't let that fool you. I am told he has the cunning of a New York stock broker. Now can you beat that combination?

★   ★   ★

Mr. _____ is a man on a quest for new ideas, new ways to preach the gospel to more people. He is a man of deep religious convictions. His style of preaching will surprise you so please don't miss a single message.

★   ★   ★

A small girl was asking her mother endless questions. "Where were you born mommie?" She asked.

"In Oklahoma." The mother replied.

"Where was daddy born?"

"In Alabama."

"And I was born in California," the little girl pondered. "I wonder how we three ever got together."

Now if you wonder how we happened to have this Evangelist from _____ in our church this week, be sure to attend the services and before the week is finished you will know.

★   ★   ★

When I met Rev. _____ at the plane I was anxious to know more about him and his work as an Evangelist.

"My friends tell me you are a self-made man," I started off.

"Certainly I am not a self-made man," he told me, "I am the revised work of a wife and daughter."

We will be anxious to hear him preach and see how well his wife and daughter accomplished their work.

★   ★   ★

I guess you notice Rev. _____ has a bald head. He was troubled about this when he first lost his hair, now he just takes it in stride. He tells me women can never be man's equal until they can sport a large bald spot on the top of their heads and still think themselves handsome.

★   ★   ★

We have heard so many wonderful reports of revival meetings our Evangelist has held. We have prayed and anticipated this time in the life of our church.

Regardless of all the great revivals Brother _____ has held, we cannot have a great meeting unless we come and work. Someone has aptly said;

> Not a truth has to earth been given,
> But brows have ached for it and souls have striven.

Won't you come and hear this good man during these services?

★   ★   ★

Our Evangelist is a man of magnificent gifts, all of them devoted to service of his fellow man.

... For Medical Doctors

Dr. _____ has lived in our city for some years now and has made a place in our hearts. He is known as a good doctor and many depend upon him for keeping them healthy. When he first graduated from medical school and came to open an office he was not sure he would succeed.

One of his first patients was a man who had broken out in a rash from head to foot. The good doctor looked him over and excused himself for a moment. Going into the back room he opened his medical book and began to look for a name to put on the rash. Failing to find one he went back to his patient. In a very professional voice he asked, "Have you ever had this before?"

"Oh, yes, three times," the patient replied.

"Well you've got it again," the doctor told him.

We are glad to have Dr. _____ to speak to us again. He is kind to take time from his very busy schedule to attend our meeting.

★ ★ ★

Our speaker this evening is fast becoming famous for his treatment of rare diseases. The other day Mrs. Smith was dressing her small daughter for a trip to Dr. _____ office.

"Now don't be frightened dear," Mrs. Smith told her, "We are only going for a checkup."

"Mommie are you sure he knows how to cure checkups?"

★ ★ ★

Dr. _____ is famous for the jokes he tells. If you feel depressed I assure you, you will go away with a smile and in a cheerful mood.

The other day Dr. _____ was making his rounds out at the mental hospital. One of the ladies rushed up to him.

"Oh Doctor, I like you so much better than the Doctor we had last year."

"Why is that, dear lady?" He asked.

"You seem just like one of us."

Now Dr. _____ is one of us tonight. Listen carefully to his message and make him feel at home afterwards.

★ ★ ★

We have for our speaker a man of high moral values. A man who is constantly studying new advances in his profession. Only eternity will reveal the many good deeds to which he has given his time in the past years.

Dr. _____ began his career in _____ but we are happy he decided to make a change and come to our fine city.

★ ★ ★

Dr. _____ received his early education in _____. After High School he attended _____ University. A burning desire to help mankind through the practice of medicine sent him on to _____ for a degree in _____. Just to see his smile in the sick room makes a patient feel better.

★ ★ ★

Dr. _____ is one doctor with his heart right side up. He finds time for so many things besides his regular practice. The ones who are absent tonight will miss a great opportunity to hear one well read and trained in some of the outstanding medical problems of our times.

The matter of witnessing should be the first concern of every Christian. Dr. _____ not only spends time telling others of a better way but he spends money helping spread the word.

His pastor tells me he is always available when called on to help in projects of the church. We are indeed glad for an opportunity to hear Dr. _____ at this time.

★ ★ ★

Dr. _____ is known as a world traveler, a writer of

medical articles, a good surgeon, and just a very fine man. He is connected with the ＿＿＿＿＿ Hospital. Dr. ＿＿＿＿＿ believes his talent for surgery is a God-given trust and it is well known that he asks for God's help as he operates. We are so glad to welcome him as our special guest tonight.

★   ★   ★

We know that there must be much trust if we are to live and be happy in this modern world. If there is one person we must trust more than others, it is our family doctor. Our speaker for this hour is just such a trusted family doctor. In his city he is lovingly referred to as Doctor ＿＿＿＿＿. Many children have grown up under his care and now trust the health of their little ones to his knowledge.

. . . For Prize Winners

Everyone likes to know a winner! We admire the person who takes first prize in any contest. Many people when they become winners and their names are on many lips, forget the power that gave them the ability to win.

We are to hear one speak today who is still a strong witness for Christ. He has won many contests and favors in the athletic world, yet he still takes time to go about and speak, trying to encourage and lift up other young people.

★   ★   ★

Mr. _____ is what is known in religious circles as a Preacher's Kid. The wonderful thing about him is he forgot to be mean and get in trouble. He was always trying to win as a ball player. He did win! He still trusts in the God of his parents. He is still anxious to set the right example for the ones who might be watching his life. He is truly a winner, in more ways than just on the playing field. He is a winner in life, choosing to live for the right.

★   ★   ★

We are glad and honored today to introduce one who has for a number of years made his home in our city. We have known for a long time he was a man of great talent but now he is being recognized by the public in general. It takes a contest at times to separate the ordinary from the extraordinary. We are very proud and delighted to have as our speaker, winner of first prize, Mr. _____.

★   ★   ★

We want you to have the opportunity to receive a blessing from meeting and hearing speak, one who has distinguished himself in the literary world. He has written exclusive features for magazines and newspapers. He is listed in the *Who's Who of American Colleges.*

32

It took many long years and much midnight oil burning to achieve the degrees awarded this man. He is an example we may point to with pride, of our American Educational system.

★   ★   ★

A leader in any field, sports, literary, medicine, or others, always sets out toward a goal. He keeps his eye on the goal. Often there are things which would distract. One who wins keeps looking forward. Our speaker is just such a person. He has won recognition in his field but already he is planning and seeking to reach for higher goals.

★   ★   ★

Congratulations to _____ for being a winner! Some one of old said, "All the world loves a lover."

In this day and age of competition in every phase of life, I say, "All the world loves a winner."

The preparation and presentation of his prize winning speech was masterful. From my own knowledge of this man I have found him to be a man of great spirit, deep compassion, true loyalty, and much consecration.

. . . For Missionaries

A Sunday School teacher was asking her small pupils to bring some of their outgrown clothes for a mission box.

"I am sorry, teacher," one small boy said, "my grandmother visited us last week and she took all our old clothes to a foreign country."

"What country has she gone to dear?" asked the teacher.

"I think she said Georgia." (Use any state the visitor might be from.)

Our beloved Missionary is one who promotes and practices missions among the people in a real foreign country.

He has been in _____ for _____ years and will return there when his furlough here is finished. Luxury is an unknown word in the land where _____ serves. He must sacrifice many things we enjoy each day, in order to preach and teach in this foreign land. I feel as if I should say, "We are in the presence of a true man of God."

★   ★   ★

If you lived in a country where there was wide-spread deprivation and suffering, wouldn't you like to meet a man who looked and smiled like our missionary speaker!

Mr. _____ has spent a number of years trying to preach the gospel to the people of _____. He offers man the possibility of new life, a life with greater social and spiritual dimensions. He is not a missionary because he is self-seeking. His aim is to bring real peace and uplift.

★   ★   ★

It was like an electric shock to the village of _____ in _____ when our beloved missionary _____ arrived there _____ ago.

They did not immediately trust him but they were excited about him. His actions were curious and I am sure he will

34

tell you some stories about their reaction to the way he spoke and abused their language. It is lucky for him that all people understand the language of love. That is a language he speaks very eloquently.

We are so glad to have you in our church. We hope we will feel the shock of your message enough to stand behind you more than ever when you return to your field of service.

★　　★　　★

Only one conclusion is possible when a man leaves his homeland and goes out to a foreign land to preach the gospel. He feels a Divine call to make such a sacrifice. He has a real love for a lost and needy world. We are so glad to have for our messenger today, Mr. _____ a missionary home from _____.

★　　★　　★

Part of a song goes; "I have a joy, joy, joy, joy, down in my heart to-day."

We have a joy in our hearts because our missionary has returned home safely from a far country. He spreads joy wherever he goes. His lovely family lived through some trying experiencees but they never lost faith in the God who called their loved one to serve. We are glad to hear some of his experiences at this time.

★　　★　　★

We all, at times, wish we could be pioneers in some endeavor. Our speaker, _____ went out to the hill country to see about starting a mission church.

High up in the mountains she saw a woman sitting on a front porch. She parked her car and walked over to speak to the woman.

"Madam, are there any Evangelicals in this section?" She asked the one who was rocking.

"I don't know for sure," the reply came, "but if there have

been any you'll find their hides nailed to the barn door. My husband is a crack shot."

We are honored to have her speak for us.

★ ★ ★

I wish it were possible for us to give a hearty word of gratitude to each woman who proclaims the Word of God in regions far away from home. We have no way of calculating the number of hours they spend in dedicated effort.

We are blessed indeed to have one of the very finest of our lady missionaries to speak at this meeting. She is only home for a few months and there are many calls on her.

A smart fellow the other day said, "Can you prove God?" "When I look at the sacrificial life of our missionaries I see the love of God," I replied.

Hear God's messenger prayerfully and reverently.

★ ★ ★

Mr. _____ faces increasing difficulty in preaching a gospel which is relevant to the times in which our youth lives. He spares no punches and his preaching has brought great results in the past. Be sure to attend and encourage your teen-agers to bring their friends.

★ ★ ★

Dr. _____ is here to lead us in our Spring Crusade for Christ. God has smiled on us by making it possible for Dr. _____ to be here and share his ministry with us. He is a choice preacher of the gospel.

★ ★ ★

Heaven will come down to earth if you hear the burning sermons of _____ during our services this week.

In great auditoriums across the nation he has drawn fabulous crowds. _____ is a master pulpiteer but he also loves the Lord and is dedicated wholly to His service.

★ ★ ★

Since I have known _____ I have found in him an extraordinary accent of authority, coupled with humility. He immediately attracts attention because he is good looking. He keeps attention because he has a heart on fire for God. He places emphasis on the fullness of the Holy Spirit.

I promise that all who attend these services and hear this great preacher will find their life changed.

. . . For Women

A hundred years ago a Mr. Law wrote: "Devotion is neither private nor public prayer, but a life given to God."

Mrs. _____ is truly a young woman who has given her life to God. While teachers in America are complaining of small salaries, and women with nothing to do are marching for causes, she is far away from home and loved ones, working to bring in the Kingdom of God.

★　★　★

Miss _____ is a missionary nurse. She serves in the country of _____. This morning when I looked out my window I saw a beautiful flower blooming. It gave me a vision of beauty in a brown dusty world. I believe, to the people who are suffering and in need in the land of _____, Miss _____ must look like a beautiful flower. If you found yourself for the first time in a clean bed, with a beautiful nurse taking care of you, wouldn't you be eager to know more about her and the Christianity she represents? We are indeed eager to hear more of your work and experiences.

★　★　★

We are going to hear a message from one who believes that living is getting involved. She is spending her life as a mission worker because she wants to excite people about Christ. She has put positive action into her religious activities.

★　★　★

I heard Miss _____ was a self-made woman, but she assures me she owes all her success to the combined efforts of her family, teachers, and friends. At any rate, we are honored to have her as our guest today. I, for one, think she is one of the greatest women in our State.

★　★　★

Mrs. _____ is the wife of our distinguished _____.
He assures me she is the power behind his successful life.
She has never been known to push herself, but all of us have
at times heard her say many words on behalf of her husband.

Mrs. _____ is a well-educated woman, a wonderful
mother, and a member of _____ Church. Her life is so
filled with good causes she never has time to complain.

I present to you _____.

★　　★　　★

_____ early showed signs of talents in writing. When
she finished school she rushed out to find a job as a journal-
ist. She was not yet satisfied so she started sitting up late
nights writing a book. Now we are glad to say she has made
a success in both fields.

★　　★　　★

Miss _____ is a poet of some distinction. She is famous for her easy, polished style of writing poetry. On the
speakers platform she is just as graceful and polished as her
poems. We are eager to hear her lecture.

★　　★　　★

The welcome mat is out! This is our way of greeting the
new members in our organization this year. Nothing excites
us so much as welcoming our new members at the beginning
of a new season.

We hope each of you will like our club and find a place
of service among us.

★　　★　　★

Miss _____, our very capable speaker for this meeting
reminds me of a quote from Oliver Wendell Holmes: "I find
the great thing in this world is not so much where we stand,
as in what direction we are going."

Our speaker knows where she stands and she has some
very definite goals she is going to reach.

★　　★　　★

This is no time for anemic efforts at doing good. We must do our best. Mrs. _____ will speak to us about how we can put forth our best effort as we approach a new year. We have consecrated and concerned women in our group.

It is indeed fortunate that one so trained and gifted could be our guest speaker this evening.

★   ★   ★

When you hear Miss _____ speak, you have the feeling that happiness has moved right in with you and will stay awhile. She is a person filled with real enthusiasm and spreads the joy of her accomplishments to others.

Starters for Introductions

This . morning I walked around my rose bushes looking for the very fairest rose to place on our breakfast table. I was well pleased with my choice and the rest of the family also seemed pleased.

When our committee was assigned the task of securing a speaker for this ocasion, we looked at the names and records of many people. Then we selected _____. We feel we chose the best and we think you will have the same feeling at the close of the evening.

★　　★　　★

An old ballad starts off,
　　"O where hae ye been, Lord Randal, my son?
　　O where hae ye been, my handsome young man?"
I feel tempted to say to our guest speaker, "O where have you been?"

We have waited almost a year for him to have an open date for us. We are happy at last to have such a fine young man as our lecturer.

★　　★　　★

We live in a day of rapid progress. New methods, new inventions, new space exploration are being discovered each day. Mr. _____ is a man who lives enthusiastically for each new step in man's advance. He will tell us about his field of work at this time.

★　　★　　★

Some people are supreme statesmen. Some are supreme in science, art, or literature. Our visiting speaker is supreme in a more unique field than any of the ones mentioned. We cannot place a yardstick beside the door and say, "Here is his exact measure of greatness."

Mr. _____ has devoted his life to the hard work of trying to make our world a better place in which to live.

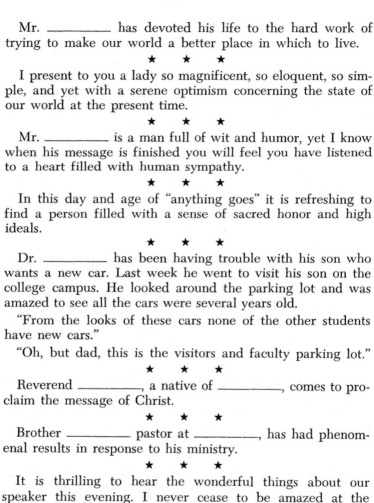

* * *

I present to you a lady so magnificent, so eloquent, so simple, and yet with a serene optimism concerning the state of our world at the present time.

* * *

Mr. _____ is a man full of wit and humor, yet I know when his message is finished you will feel you have listened to a heart filled with human sympathy.

* * *

In this day and age of "anything goes" it is refreshing to find a person filled with a sense of sacred honor and high ideals.

* * *

Dr. _____ has been having trouble with his son who wants a new car. Last week he went to visit his son on the college campus. He looked around the parking lot and was amazed to see all the cars were several years old.

"From the looks of these cars none of the other students have new cars."

"Oh, but dad, this is the visitors and faculty parking lot."

* * *

Reverend _____, a native of _____, comes to proclaim the message of Christ.

* * *

Brother _____ pastor at _____, has had phenomenal results in response to his ministry.

* * *

It is thrilling to hear the wonderful things about our speaker this evening. I never cease to be amazed at the glory and grace of our foreign missionaries.

* * *

Mr. _____ is an outstanding musician. You will want to be in the choir and enjoy his directing. You will want to be in the congregation and enjoy his solos.

★ ★ ★

Here is a man known for his beautiful, glorious voice.

★ ★ ★

Can anything be more inspiring than to hear a firsthand report from our mission work? That is just what we expect tonight from _____.

★ ★ ★

Dr. _____ preaches for numbers! I am glad. It might be my boy or my girl left out if he just worked for a chosen few. Yes, let us help him reach all the numbers we can!

★ ★ ★

The secret behind _____ popularity as a speaker is the fact that he speaks up, and shuts up on time.

★ ★ ★

Mr. _____ is an outspoken Christian. He is a successful business man but he presents the claims of Jesus Christ in a dynamic way.

★ ★ ★

Our featured speaker is a friend of students. He works at understanding their problems. He believes in listening to those who need help and then helping.

★ ★ ★

It is a happy occasion when I can give special recognition to an old friend and former classmate.

★ ★ ★

This is a delightful experience, to be able to say a few words about my former professor. I would not have dared say much back in my college days. We held our beloved professor in high esteem.

★ ★ ★

We salute a man at this time who has accomplished a good work. We owe him our deepest gratitude as a church and as a denomination.

★   ★   ★

When _____ was young he heard someone say of his life: "My Lord has need of it." He immediately began to give his life and work to the service of God.

★   ★   ★

Mr. _____ is a participating member of this church. Yet he goes about over our territory speaking. We had to make plans far ahead to secure him for this meeting.

Replies to Introductions

I want to thank the pastor of this church for inviting me to share this service with you. You have given me a very gracious and overwhelming welcome. It is not often I am asked to go so far away from home as to your lovely state. I think some of God's finest people live here. I hope to meet many of you personally at the close of the service.

★   ★   ★

Well, I'm glad I'm here! The attendance looks great. When I walked off the plane I met a small girl. She was so pretty I wanted to talk to her a moment so I said a few words.

"Why are you here?" she asked.

"I want to tell people about God," I replied.

"Oh, I've heard about him," she told me. "He goes to our church."

Now I hope He is here in this church tonight. We want to feel His presence.

★   ★   ★

Brother _____ has been so nice to introduce me in such glowing terms. I spoke to his small son before the service.

"Which lady is your mother?" I asked.

"Mother is the one who's hair is all waves, and daddy is the one who's head is all beach."

"Well, they are a fine couple and you are fortunate to have them as your church leaders.

★   ★   ★

Thank you for the kind introduction. You were nice to call me Dr. _____. Well I am not a doctor, I'm not even a registered nurse.

★   ★   ★

The subject I have been assigned tonight is so great and has such a wide scope I feel like a Fox Terrier trying to attack a grisly bear.

★   ★   ★

A friend asked an unemployed man: "Why don't you go to work? Are you afraid of work?"

"No, I can lay right down beside it and go to sleep."

Tonight I want us to ask ourselves why as a denomination we are not going to work?

★   ★   ★

Try to do the things that Jesus Christ would do,
If He were here on earth in place of you.
Would He be snappy, cross, or mean?
Would He be seen in places Christians are too
    often found?

If you see discouraged ones, must you pass them by?
Try offering them courage, a hope that Christ can give,
A purpose and a blessing to everyone who lives.

★   ★   ★

When faith goes to market it always takes a large basket. I have with me my largest basket. I expect to see great out-pourings of God's love this week.

★   ★   ★

It is a joy to be back in your lovely church again. You have been so generous in your welcome. The arrangements for my physical well-being while I am here are superb. I cannot say enough about the joy I have experienced as I spent time with your dedicated pastor planning these meetings.

★   ★   ★

A new lady taxi driver brought me from the station. I know she was new because a traffic policeman stopped us on the way.

"Didn't you see that red light?" he asked her.

"Oh, yes, I saw it, but when you've seen one you've seen them all."

I have visited many churches but none seem so warm and friendly as yours. You do indeed live up to your reputation of friendliness.

★　　★　　★

What graciousness you have demonstrated! I feel very much at home in your midst. I want to thank you sincerely for giving me this opportunity to tell of my experiences and how God has lifted me from sin and made me a useful vessel.

★　　★　　★

In introducing me Mr. _____ made some clever and penetrating observations. Now I must make some in reply. I rode down here in Mr. _____ new car. He was out looking at cars the other day. The salesman showed him one that looked promising. "What makes it jerk so when it starts?" The salesman replied, "Just shows it is a good car and anxious to get started." I guess I should get started.

★　　★　　★

It is always a pleasure to be introduced by someone so gracious and kind as _____. I hope you will get a spiritual and a psychological lift from my message tonight. I have already received a blessing from meeting and talking with so many of you.

★　　★　　★

How wonderful it is to have friends who will make such glamorous introductions! Any one should be able to speak after such kind words.

I hope our motto during these services together will be found in Acts 5:42.

> "And daily in the temple, and
> in every house, they ceased not
> to teach and preach Jesus. . . ."

★　　★　　★

Since my arrival in your community yesterday, your good pastor has shown solicitous and tender concern for my comfort. The demensions of his kindness know no bounds. I came hoping to receive a blessing and to bring a blessing. Now I have already been blessed by just feeling your gracious kindness and love.

★　★　★

Your kind president is unquestionably the nicest person I have met in some time. You may be sure after he gave me such an illustrious introduction I will be his life-long admirer.

★　★　★

I felt despair in my heart when I came to your lovely city. In your church I have found a veritable oasis of encouragment. You seem to have as your aim and purpose the preserving of your Christian faith. May God continue to bless you in this endeavor.

Every place I go I hear about the terrible condition of our world today. Here I have been met by a people who are striving to make the world better. Thank you for asking me to speak tonight.

★　★　★

There is an old saying, "Never judge a man until you have walked two weeks in his moccasins." I don't believe I could walk two weeks in the shoes of your pastor. I never saw such a man for getting around a town. He is very fine and I count it an honor to be asked to speak from his pulpit. It takes a great people to back up a great man and he assures me you are just that.

★　★　★

From a heart filled with gratitude I wish to thank you for the beautiful music we have already enjoyed. I felt so inspired I could scarcely wait for my turn to praise God. This service has been one of beauty and perfection thus far. I will be everlastingly grateful for the opportunity of being a part of this service.

★　　★　　★

Thank you for your gracious welcome. I shall be everlastingly grateful for the friendship of your pastor. He has been kind to invite me to your church and to entertain me in his Christian home.

★　　★　　★

After my long ride I felt like a frog on the freeway with his hopper busted. After a few minutes of refreshing conversation with your pastor I could not restrain myself, I was repaired and all ready to visit a church he recommended so highly.

★　　★　　★

I am reminded, looking at this congregation, of a small boy who went to answer the doorbell. There stood an elderly lady.

"Johnny, you don't know me, do you? I am your grandmother on your father's side."

"Shucks, you won't be here ten minutes until you'll see you are on the wrong side."

What is wrong with these front seats? Let us make an effort to get someone on their side tomorrow night.

★　　★　　★

Thank you Mr. _____ for such a warm welcome. I hope as we work together for a few days we can put the key of God's love in every door of this community.

I am impressed with the life and zeal I have found in this congregation. At times I am asked to speak in churches which are so dead the termites are holding hands to keep the building from falling down.

★　　★　　★

I started preaching on the street corner of a city near my home town. I gave my introduction ten times before I ever got a group to stay long enough to hear my first point. I never did get to point number two.

Now tonight you are a captive audience. I'll enjoy giving you all my points.

★ ★ ★

I come to you as a plain man. I have not led any demonstrations, I have not even gone on strike for higher wages. I just try to spend my time telling a lost world about a Christ who will save.

★ ★ ★

Your pastor and staff have given me a royal welcome. They have shown me how they have organized for the task of soul-winning. I feel highly honored to be a part of your church organization for a week of intense activity.

★ ★ ★

This seems to be a day of investments. People invest in land, in stocks and bonds, in homes, cars, and furniture. Tonight I am going to let you in on some first-hand information about an investment that will never stop paying dividends. It will reward you with a beautiful mansion and no worry about upkeep or taxes. Could you think of a better investment?

Listen carefully while I give you the particulars.

Replies for People with a Distinct Feature

The other day Mrs. _____ heard her husband singing a little rhyme written by Addison Hallock, it ran like this:

> Past my prime, and I behold
> No silver threads among the gold;
> Mirror, mirror on the wall,
> I behold no threads at all.

He does lack a few grey hairs on his head but I like him just the same after he gave me such a nice introduction.

★ ★ ★

Mr. _____ has been married a year now. We all wondered when he fell in love how the marriage would work out. After all, he was the most eligible bachelor in our denomination for a number of years. His sweet, pretty wife gave me the answer when I met her today.

"We agreed that when we disagreed on something we would get in the car and drive around sightseeing for awhile before we reached a decision."

"Well how did it work out?" I asked her.

"At the end of the first year we wholeheartedly agreed we had driven the car so much we needed a new one."

★ ★ ★

Dr. Peter McLeod, pastor of a church in Waco, Texas told the following: A man and his wife had been married fifty years. They were a beef-stew couple. He was always beefing about something and she was always stewing. One day some of the children persuaded them to go to a psychologist. They were having one of their very worst arguments at the time. When they were ushered into the Doctor's office the woman kept talking as fast as she could for fifteen minutes. After trying several times to get her attention the doctor got up from his chair and went to her side. He kissed her thoroughly.

"Now, husband, she should have that treatment about three times a week," the doctor told him.

"Alright, doctor if you say so. I'll bring her back three times a week."

★   ★   ★

I am here to speak and you are here to listen. If you get through before I do, let me know by raising your hand. But, please, give me a head start to begin with.

★   ★   ★

I have heard it said of Mr. _____ that he makes the audience sit up and take notice. Well, I am afraid I often make them slump over and go to sleep. With a subject such as we have this evening only a very dull person could go to sleep. You know your own capacity.

★   ★   ★

As some rare perfume in a vase of clay
    Pervades it with a fragrance not its own,
So when thou dwellest in a mortal soul,
    All heaven's own sweetness seems around it thrown.
— Stowe

It is worth a trip to your city just to hear the sweet way your pastor introduces a guest.

Words of Farewell

In behalf of our Sunday School I would like to express our appreciation for the years of service Mr. _____ has so faithfully rendered in our church.

There will be a vacant place when he goes away. We must rededicate and redouble our efforts to make our work grow.

He has certainly set us an example of unselfishness. He never semed to complain when we imposed on his good nature.

We certainly tell you good-bye with regret. Our best wishes go with you in your new place of service.

★   ★   ★

As you leave our church we would like to express our appreciation for your years of faithful service and leadership.

May God's blessings and His guidance be ever with you is our sincere prayer.

★   ★   ★

It has been a pleasure to be associated with a man of true humility, culture and spiritual values these past years. It is with regret we come to bid him farewell.

★   ★   ★

Thank God men can grow! We have seen our pastor grow from a young man just out of school into a fine leader and wonderful preacher. We come now to see him leave us because he is still growing. He goes to a larger field. We will follow him with our prayers and best wishes.

★   ★   ★

During his tenure as president of our convention Dr. _____ has met the supreme test of a truly great man. He has led us in sound beliefs and practices. He has not ducked controversy. We are especially grateful to him for the time and effort he has given these past years to our denomination. We know that he feels he must have a rest from such pressing duties, but he will be behind our newly elected president all the way.

Thank you Dr. _____ and we will always love and respect you for the great leader you are.

★   ★   ★

We come to bid farewell today to a leader of great ability. He is an independent and profound thinker. He has demonstrated a wide knowledge, a clarity of thought and careful development of leaders.

He has set us an example of deep conviction and has given us the advantage of his wide experience. Under his leadership our denomination has prospered. We feel he is leaving a large place to be filled but we would not deny him a lighter load. Or will it be a greater challenge?

★   ★   ★

Not only do I come today to pay farewell tribute to our pastor but to one who has been a good friend to all. Thank God for sending him our way. His work has been superb. It is with regret we accept his resignation.

★   ★   ★

The one who leaves us today to move to a larger field has made a signal contribution to our organization during his tenure in office. He has not hesitated to take a firm stand on important issues. We respect and admire him. As he finds new avenues of service we will be listening for the reports of his progress.

★   ★   ★

For the past _____ years it has been the joy and privilege of the employees in this office to be closely associated with Mr. _____. He has always been a part of our team and we never found him lacking in a spirit of cooperation.

We appreciate him for his abilities. He is a warm and sincere person. We will miss him as a friend and as a fellow worker.

★　★　★

In the shadow of this great man's influence I have grown as a Christian. In a commercialized world he has shown all of us there is a greater love than that of success and money.

We wish for him to have many days ahead filled with pleasure in service and life.

★　★　★

My admiration and respect for this man has continued to grow throughout the years of our association. It is hard to bid "good-bye" to one we have worked with so closely and upon whom we have often leaned heavily in times of decision making.

★　★　★

Words of Farewell
No, children, not another one!
  I've told you all the rhymes I know.
Go off to play and be content,
  And do not tease good nature so.

My breath is gone, my eyes are dim,
  Too many stories have I told.
But if I've made you happy, dears,
  Within your hearts my memory hold.
Good Bye!

★　★　★

This is my last service with your church. I want to thank you for the privilege of being your guest minister this past week. You have been so kind to invite me into your homes for food and fellowship. When you are driving through my hometown please stop and say, hello.

Thanks to each of you, especially the committee members who had charge of visitation and revival arrangements.

★　★　★

Words can't begin to show the pleasure I have experienced this day as your guest speaker. I hope the future holds many good things for your church.

★   ★   ★

I am taking away from your city the very best of pleasant memories.

★   ★   ★

I often heard my parents mention they remembered a time when we had no automobile. I well remember when we had no radio. My wife remembers when we had no TV set. My son is talking about the time before we could get into orbit. What a world! I am sure many wonderful things will be forgotten as time goes on. Until the end of my life I will remember how great this evening spent with your organization has been. Thank you for inviting me.

★   ★   ★

This afternoon I will leave by plane and fly to my new mission station. I will meet many new friends and see many new sights. But always dear to my heart will be the friends in this church who are helping to make it possible for me to stay on the mission field.

Will you please remember me in your prayers? I, too, shall pray for you. I know that when I come home again there will be dear faces missing. Some will be gone to heaven. Some will merely be moved to other cities. But I will look forward to my return in _____ years.

★   ★   ★

You have entered into this meeting whole-heartedly. We have looked at some basic needs of our denomination. Now as it is time for me to bid you good-bye, I do so with a feeling of confidence that you will work to carry out the things we have learned. Thank you for a very inspiring visit to your church.

★   ★   ★

It is time for me to say goodbye to this dear congregation. You have undergirded my work and helped me in many ways. As I leave I ask you to pray for me and my family in our new field of service.

★ ★ ★

As I have worked as your leader these past years, I have studied the needs of the community and tried in a small way to meet them. You have cooperated in a great way.

Now the Lord is calling me to a new field. It is hard to leave friends we love so dearly and, with whom we have worked so closely.

We pray God to send you a new and better leader. We will be remembering you as we get started in our new work.

★ ★ ★

They tell me that the last apples on a tree are the sweetest and the mellowest. I hope this is true. I have reached the age of retirement and I feel that I must resign from my position in our church organization. From now on I must look at life from a different perspective. I have no desire to thrust myself and my views upon the younger people in leadership. I shall always pray for you. And if at any time I can be of service in counsel or judgment, please do not hesitate to call on me.

Sands of time do run out. They will for all of you. But the years that are left for me I want to be years of fulfillment. I leave you with love in my heart for all.

★ ★ ★

In farewell I would like to be able to tell all of you how very much I love you. My years of service here have been happy ones and I pray, useful ones. My family and myself have always been proud to tell people we lived in_____.

You have often filled our days with sunshine by your little and big acts of kindness.

★ ★ ★

My years on the faculty of this school have been pleasant and happy. There has been very little faculty dissatisfaction. Personally I have felt that _____ School was a small oasis of peace in a world of students torn by strife.

All teachers have to face the problem of finances when they have children of their own to educate. I am making a change because I feel I can help my family by doing so.

The school here, as well as the administration, will always remain dear to my heart.

★　★　★

Many lasting bonds of friendship have been forged between myself and the people in this office. You have all been so kind and considerate to work with.

★　★　★

If I were a poet I would write the feelings of my heart in rhyme. Since I am just a common person with no talent for writing and not much for speaking, let me say, in parting, you are just the greatest! We will surely miss each of you.

★　★　★

I was warned my speech tonight might be like one a minister delivered to a congregation after a big "dinner on the ground." When he had finished, his farewell words were, "Tonight I talked in other peoples sleep."

Thank you for staying awake, your attention was quite invigorating and helpful.

★　★　★

Tonight I felt a little like the patient who went to a young doctor to complain of a rash covering him from head to foot.

The young doctor had no idea what could be wrong. He excused himself and went into his inner office. Looking hastily in his medical books he could not find an answer.

He returned to the patient and asked, "Have you ever had this before?"

"Yes."

"Well, you've got it again," the doctor told him.

You have heard me again tonight. Each time I speak to your club I grow to like and know you better. Thanks for inviting me again.

★   ★   ★

Since my wonderful visit here on your campus I am sure I shall think of all of you each day the whole year through. If you are having one of your lively ball games, remember I am rooting for you to win. If you are having a crusade for Christ my prayers will be with you. How pleasant it is to know we have schools like this one with good, dedicated students.

★   ★   ★

After my visit in your mission group I think of a poem written by a mother, Ann Nechodom.

> Each time I clean the woodwork
> I note with wistful tear
> That fingerprints grow larger,
> Climb higher every year.

I have watched with interest as girls have become women and leaders in your organization. Now as I say farewell for another period of time I think with anticipation how some of you will have grown in the work before I return.

★   ★   ★

You have given me such a royal welcome and we have had a profitable time together. Now as it is time for me to say goodbye I will confess that as I arrived in your city I felt something like a family I read about.

They were entertaining an overnight guest. At bed time the guest went with the father and mother to hear the prayers of the five year old daughter.

"I can't think what to say, mommie," she said.

"Just say what you have heard mommie or daddy say."

"Dear Lord," prayed the child, "help us to get that big blabber-mouth to bed before midnight, Amen."

I resolved not to bore you by preaching too long. You were such an exceptional audience it took all my will power to close at the end of the first hour.

★ ★ ★

It seems only yesterday since I came to labor with you as pastor and friend. The years have been kind and I appreciate all of you and the help you have given me.

Words of Appreciation

My deepest appreciation to those who helped make our Youth Banquet a big success. The committee members are to be commended for their beautiful planning and decorating. The meal was tremendous, the entertainment was wholesome and wonderful.

★　★　★

Thanks for your prayers, cards and flowers, as well as visits during the serious illness of our beloved one.

We deeply appreciate the untiring ministry and effort of the Christian doctors. The nurses were beautiful examples of dedicated womanhood.

It was not the will of the Lord for our dear one to remain with us but the wonderful way you stood by us in these trying days made us surer than ever of a heaven.

★　★　★

Thank you for sending a telegram with assurances of your prayers. You made me feel a close link with home.

★　★　★

We are indeed grateful to our dear pastor and our fellow church members for the prayers, food, cards and visits during our great loss.

★　★　★

I deeply appreciate the anniversary party. I am proud to be called the pastor of such a wonderful group.

★　★　★

Somebody

Some-body did a golden deed,
　Proving him-self a friend in need;
Some-body sang a cheerful song,

Brightening the sky the whole day long,
Was that some-body you?

Some-body made a loving gift,
    Cheerfully tried a load to lift;
Some-body told the love of Christ,
    Told how His will was sacrificed,
Was that some-body you?

Some-body filled the days with light,
    Constantly chased away the night;
Some-body's work bore joy and peace,
    Surely his life will never cease.
Was that some-body you?
                    — John R. Clements

Yes I think that somebody was you. You have been a wonderful leader and friend. We do not have enough words to adequately express our appreciation for you and the life you have lived in our midst.

★   ★   ★

When I think of Mr. _____, I think of the great verse of Scripture found in Psalm 1:1.

Indeed he is a man who has walked uprightly in our city. He has spent much time in civic organizations and in his church, striving to make this a better place to live. We want, in just a small way, to show our appreciation for his work.

★   ★   ★

It is said of a good Boy Scout, "He carries his own pack." I know of no better words to express our appreciation for Mr. _____, than to say, "He carries his own pack and often also that of a friend."

★   ★   ★

We look to our teachers and officers with high hopes. With gratitude and thanksgiving to God for these fine consecrated men and women and for their magnificient service.

Like teacher, like class, so if your class does well it is a sign you are working as a teacher.

We appreciate the response to training programs shown by our teaching staff. You have been loyal and cooperative.

★　　★　　★

A Woman in It

They talk about a woman's sphere
As though it had a limit,
There's not a task to mankind
given;
There's not a blessing or a woe;
There's not a whispered "yes" or
"no";
There's not a life, there's not a
birth,
That has a feather's weight of
worth
Without a woman in it.

★　　★　　★

How better could we honor our mothers than to pause on one special day each year to pay tribute to her. We wish to pause and think of happy days of childhood when our mothers made life secure and happy. We could never say enough to show all our love and appreciation for the blessings our mothers gave us. All love and honor to mothers today!

★　　★　　★

We wish to express appreciation for teachers and officers who said, "Let us go on" (Mark 1:38), and have worked toward that goal.

★　　★　　★

My sincere appreciation for this lovely bouquet. Your thoughtfulness is beautiful in itself. I shall enjoy the flowers.

As I look at them and see their beauty I will also think of the beauty of the dear friends who sent them.

★   ★   ★

I have enjoyed so very much your hospitality today. You have been so helpful and kind. Now you present me with a gift. Indeed my "cup runneth over." Thank you.

★   ★   ★

I cannot express all the appreciation I feel for the loyal, faithful work my committees have shown this year. The work of our organization has gone smoothly. The credit goes to the well-functioning committees.

★   ★   ★

We appreciate so much your coming from _____ to bring us the talk of the evening. We have been inspired and awakened to our great opportunities. You will always be a welcome guest in our meetings.

★   ★   ★

May I express appreciation for all of us to the program committee. They showed supurb teamwork and cooperation in their planning. We have indeed enjoyed each program. Thank you for your very detailed planning.

Words of Wisdom
to Spice Up a Message

Those who bring sunshine to the lives of others cannot keep it from themselves. — Sir James Barrie

★   ★   ★

"Do not laugh at the fallen; there may be slippery places ahead in your own path."

★   ★   ★

"A lot of people are worrying about what is on the moon and they have no idea what is on the other side of their own town."

★   ★   ★

Whosoever putteth his trust in the Lord shall be safe.

★   ★   ★

Laziness travels so slowly that poverty soon overtakes it.

★   ★   ★

To sin by silence when they should protest makes cowards of men. — Abraham Lincoln

★   ★   ★

All power corrupts — and absolute power corrupts absolutely. — Lord Action

★   ★   ★

Of all the forces that make for a better world, none is so indispensable, none so powerful, as hope.

★   ★   ★

Some people get lost in thought because it's unfamiliar territory to them.

★   ★   ★

I have held many things in my hands, and have lost them

all; but whatever I have placed in God's hand, that I still possess. — Martin Luther

★   ★   ★

Wisdom is knowing what to do, skill is knowing how to do it, and virtue is doing it well.

★   ★   ★

A champion is a fellow who gets licked two or three times a week, and keeps right on calling himself a champion.

★   ★   ★

A fool and his money are soon spotted.

★   ★   ★

Courage is not the absence of fear — it is the mastery of it.

★   ★   ★

You are complete in Christ only when you are completely in Christ. — *Religious Telescope*

★   ★   ★

You are an old-timer if you can remember when the sky was the limit.

★   ★   ★

A pretty good marriage counselor is the tot who tries to hug Mommie and Daddy at the same time.

★   ★   ★

Try hardest when it is hardest to pray.

★   ★   ★

All roads lead to something.

★   ★   ★

The thing most needed in the American home today is the family. — Jeffrey Martin

★   ★   ★

Do not turn green with envy, it makes you ripe for trouble.

★   ★   ★

The kindness planned for tomorrow doesn't count today.

★   ★   ★

Love in action always shows up better than just love spoken.

★   ★   ★

It often has occurred to me,
Since all the world's a stage,
That one thing I would like to see
Is more folks act their age.
— S. S. Biddle

★   ★   ★

My parents straightened up wayward children by bending them over.

★   ★   ★

Music is one language in which you cannot say mean or sarcastic things.

★   ★   ★

A wise man will make more opportunities than he finds.
— Forbes

★   ★   ★

A lie travels around the world while truth is putting on her boots. — C. H. Spurgeon

★   ★   ★

As long as there are unsaved people in the community we need the church.

★   ★   ★

It seems like a long block when success is just around the corner. Keep walking.

★   ★   ★

Some people think the best drivers sit in the back seat.

★   ★   ★

When God is moving — who can hinder?

★   ★   ★

Unless we give part of ourselves away, unless we can live

with other people and understand them and help them, we are missing the most essential part of our human lives.

— Dr. H. Taylor

★ ★ ★

Be thrifty without being stingy. Be generous without being wasteful.

★ ★ ★

Our worst misfortunes never happen, and most of our miseries lie in anticipation. — De Balzac

★ ★ ★

There never was a person who did anything worth doing that did not receive more than he gave. — Beecher

★ ★ ★

The consecrated one-talent man or woman has promise of a larger influence for good than an intellectual genius who has not met the Master. — Zwemmer

★ ★ ★

There is nothing opened by mistake as often as one's mouth!

★ ★ ★

Between the great things we can't do and the little things we don't do, the danger is we shall do nothing at all.

★ ★ ★

A great man is one who remains silent when he has nothing to say.

★ ★ ★

God specializes in things that are impossible.

★ ★ ★

Freedom is not free, it is bought with a dear price.

★ ★ ★

What blessedness would ensue if we loved our neighbors as we love ourselves.

★ ★ ★

Service follows real worship.

★   ★   ★

Human minds are like wagons. When they have a light load they are much noisier than when the load is heavy.

★   ★   ★

Someone has said that a little fly in Noah's ark was just as safe as the largest elephant.

★   ★   ★

God has plenty of current, but it lights the world only when it passes through the human lamp.

★   ★   ★

Women's minds are cleaner than men's because they change them so much.

★   ★   ★

Temptation is a sign you have an adversary. The devil.

★   ★   ★

If criticism had any real power to destroy the skunk would be extinct by now. — Will Rogers

★   ★   ★

The Devil can't stand long before a good testimony.

★   ★   ★

He could strut sitting down. — Homer Martinez

★   ★   ★

Someone must care enough in marriage to patch the tears.

★   ★   ★

We start to live when we start to give.

★   ★   ★

Do nothing you would not want to be doing when Jesus comes. — Ham and Ramsey, revival team motto.

★   ★   ★

It might be puppy love but it is real to the puppy.

★   ★   ★

A sign found hanging above an old-fashioned razor-strap; "I need thee every hour."

★ ★ ★

If he had unfolded Texas just one more time it would have gone around the world. — Words of a native.

★ ★ ★

Courage is fear after one has said his prayers.

★ ★ ★

A good thing to remember,
And a brave thing to do
Is work with the construction gang
And not the wrecking crew.
                    — Miss Reeves

★ ★ ★

It is no disgrace to fail when trying. The one time you don't want to fail is the last time you try. — Charles Kettering

★ ★ ★

The typical husband is one who lays down the law to his wife and then accepts all her amendments. — F. G. Kernan

★ ★ ★

If kids didn't ask questions, they'd never learn how little their parents know! — The man on Ave. Q

★ ★ ★

The most wasted day — one which we have not laughed.
                    — Chamfort

★ ★ ★

The man who removes a mountain begins by carrying away small stones. — Confucious

★ ★ ★

You can't control the other fellow's opportunities, but you can grasp your own. — *The Word and Way*

★ ★ ★

A friend is the first person who comes in when the whole world has gone out. — Bulwer-Lytton.

★　★　★

It would make better people of us if we thought about other people's faults while we were asleep and about our own faults while we are awake.

★　★　★

Sin often begins as "fun."

★　★　★

Keep your fears to yourself, but share your courage with others. — Robert Louis Stevenson

★　★　★

A knife-wound heals, but a tongue-wound festers.

★　★　★

Civility costs nothing, and buys everything.

— Lady Montague

★　★　★

An open door invites callers.

★　★　★

Liberty is one thing you can't have unless you give it to others.

★　★　★

In company keep a short tongue.

★　★　★

Everybody agrees, true humility is a wonderful trait and it's a funny thing more of us don't give it a trial.

★　★　★

Beauty passes; wisdom remains.

★　★　★

Popularity comes from pleasing people, but greatness comes from pleasing God.

★　★　★

A college education is no longer a luxury we hope we can afford our children. It is a necessity of life.

★　★　★

Honor is the reward for what we give, not what we receive.

★　★　★

No one ever climbed the ladder of success with his hands in his pockets.

★　★　★

Man can climb a ladder of success if he has a good wife to hold it steady.

★　★　★

Failure comes in can'ts, success comes in cans.

★　★　★

Never pick a parking place when you are on the highway of success.

★　★　★

If you can recall when homes had feather dusters you are an oldtimer.

★　★　★

A short man looks taller to the girl he is with if she knows he is sitting on a well-filled wallet.

★　★　★

Don't skim your milk of human kindness.

★　★　★

Stairs are climbed step by step. Many things come day by day.

★　★　★

I have but one candle to burn, and would rather burn it out where people are dying in darkness, than in a land which is flooded with light. — A missionary

★　★　★

Wisdom is knowing what to do next, skill is knowing how to do it; and virtue is doing it. — David Starr Jordan

No man can give what he has not.

* * *

Valor is to travel on an ocean liner without tipping. Discretion is to come back on a different ship.

* * *

Those who do not forgive others should never sin themselves.

* * *

All the water in the sea will not sink a ship until it gets inside.

* * *

Dignity does not consist in possessing honors, but in deserving them.

* * *

A world without a Sabbath would be like a man without a smile, like a homestead without a garden. It is the joyous day of the whole week. — Beecher

* * *

To think about troubles is to waste your own time — to talk about them is to waste other people's time. — Beecher

* * *

The world is at the crossroads and the signs are all down. Which way shall we go?

* * *

A dishonest gain brings pain for all time to come.

* * *

My wife often shows little or no interest in what I am saying — unless I happen to be saying it to another woman.

* * *

As every thread of gold is valuable, so is every minute of time.

* * *

Each day should be a mountain peak of hope.

Some teaching is merely the exchange of ignorance.

★　　★　　★

Prayer is man's highest privilege.

★　　★　　★

Throw your heart over the bar and your body will follow.

★　　★　　★

Ye are the light of the world. Go shine for me.

★　　★　　★

Go as far as you can see, and when you get there you'll see farther. — Elbert Hubbard

★　　★　　★

Never let difficulty stop you. It may be only sand on your track to keep you from skidding.

Bits of Humor

Such a large audience frightens me. I hope I don't make the mistake one of my friends made. He got up to preach on Samson and was so nervous he called him Tarzan all the way through the sermon.

★   ★   ★

I am glad to see you. I have been away on a vacation. Do you know the definition of a vacation?

It consists of 2 weeks
which are 2 short.
After which you are 2 tired
2 return to work
And 2 broke not 2.

★   ★   ★

A friend stopped me on the street this morning and asked about my vacation. Did you fish with flies? he said.

"Fish with flies!" I said, "we fished with them, ate with them, and slept with them."

★   ★   ★

My teen-ager told me the other day, "Mother says mixed greens are good for one."

"Why, yes, I am sure they are," I replied.

"Well good, I'd like some fives, tens, and twenties."

★   ★   ★

My notes seem to have gotten mixed up, but not as mixed up as the maid whose mistress sent her to see about a cake in the oven.

"Stick the knife in and see if it comes out clean."

After a few moments the maid returned to the room. "Madam the knife came out just as clean as could be so I gathered up all the other dirty knives and stuck them in the cake also."

★ ★ ★

A mother finding herself with an extraordinarily wild group of children at a birthday party made an announcement.

"There will be a special prize for the first three to go home."

Now I am not going to give any prizes but I will try to send you home early.

★ ★ ★

Some of you have heard about my new grandson. I tell you I am proud of that grandchild but my problem is how to get used to sleeping with a grandmother.

★ ★ ★

My message sometimes gets longer or shorter according to the mood of the audience. I met a boy the other night in the drug store. He bought a one pound box of candy, a two pound box of candy, and a five pound box of candy.

"Do you have three girls?" I asked him.

"No I just have one girl, if she just asks me to come in I will give her the one pound box. If she lets me hold her hand I will give her the two pound box. But if she lets me kiss her I will give her the five pound box."

★ ★ ★

Diets are very popular today. Every one wants a diet that will make them more beautiful and more healthful.

The other day a man went into a store and bought a large quantity of pins and needles.

"Going to start sewing?" the Clerk asked him.

"No, I'm a sword swallower and I'm going on a diet."

★ ★ ★

A man came home to find his wife had been having an argument with the light company.

76

"Who won?" he asked.

"It was a draw." She replied, "We don't get any light and they don't get any money."

★   ★   ★

Sometimes we have so many meetings at our church I feel like a pilot.

"How are we doing?" A passenger asked the pilot of a small private plane.

"We're lost but we're making good time," replied the pilot.

Are we losing the goal for which all churches should strive?

★   ★   ★

Parents are sometimes as careless with their children as Sue was with her clothes.

Sue was taking a cruise vacation. "My cabin is so nice," she told her friend. "But I didn't like the washing machine on the wall."

"There wasn't any washing machine on the wall, that was a port-hole."

"Oh, then that is why none of my clothes ever came back."

Better take stock of where you are sending your children or they might not return.

★   ★   ★

We want to honor our graduates today. They are all fine and have worked hard. One of them was known to rush out of the graduation exercises and shout, "Here I am world. I have an A.B."

The world looked at him with a smile and replied, "Now you are ready to start learning the hard part of the alphabet."

★   ★   ★

Many ministers today are putting their ammunition to the wrong use.

The other day a man went into a drug store he often frequented.

"Did you kill many moths with the mothballs I sold you? the clerk asked.

"No, I tried for hours but I threw all the balls away and didn't hit a moth."

★ ★ ★

Some people are working for the wrong thing and will probably be disapppointed in the rewards.

Joe had a rich aunt. He spent years of his life pretending he was fond of his aunt and her twenty cats. When she died, all her money went to charity and all her cats went to Joe.

★ ★ ★

Now if you are going to tear me and my speech to pieces I think I will do like the man who went into the barber shop.

The barber nicked him badly as he shaved him. Hoping to restore the man's feeling of well-being, the barber asked, "Do you want your head wrapped in a hot towel?"

"No, thanks," the customer replied. "I'll carry it home under my arm."

★ ★ ★

Are you sure your wife is expecting me for dinner?

Expecting you! I should say so. This morning we argued about it for half an hour.

★ ★ ★

This has been such a good program so far. I feel almost like a College President about whom I heard. A mother trying to enroll her son in college asked, "Won't it help his admissions exams because he is so good on the rock-and-roll guitar?"

"It might have helped five years ago," the president replied, "now we are looking for a few listeners."

★ ★ ★

The other day I decided I must be middle aged. The tele-

78

phone rang on Saturday night and I hoped it was not for me.

★ ★ ★

I must be middle-aged, the cops all look so young now.

Invitations

. . . Public

Come join our group next _____ and enjoy a day of food, fun, and fellowship in the park. We will have plenty of transportation. Just be here promptly at _____ with a picnic lunch.

★   ★   ★

Be sure to attend the play in our church fellowship hall next _____. Our youth will be the talented actors. They will make history come alive for you.

★   ★   ★

I want to take this time to call your attention to a new program. Our church services will be broadcast each week at _____ o'clock, over _____ station. Never be absent unless you must but tell your friends who are shut in about this program. They will want to worship with us.

★   ★   ★

Do you want to be happy? Happiness is attending the Family Night Supper. Don't miss. All members are invited.

★   ★   ★

"It is not necessary for you to be in a key position before you can unlock the door of opportunity."

★   ★   ★

We expect you to unlock that door by attending our Silver Tea next _____. All the proceeds will go to help us furnish our new church kitchen.

. . . Church

We extend a cordial invitation to you and your congregation to attend an Easter Sunrise Service.

★　★　★

We would welcome you and your church members to participate in a meaningful service next _____ night. Dr. _____ will be the guest speaker. He is a world traveler and will show some slides.

★　★　★

Come visit our services Sunday. In our church you will find light for the dark shadows of your life. You will find a friend who will be closer than a brother. Can you neglect so great an invitation?

★　★　★

Is your appointment calendar full? Please make room for one more apointment. This might be the most important date you ever kept. Come hear Mr. _____ speak. He will be in _____ Church on Friday evening at 7:00 P.M.

★　★　★

Will you accept a paid up life insurance policy? You must believe that Jesus Christ died for your sins.

. . . Letters

May be extend a cordial invitation to you and your congregation to attend our city-wide Easter Sunrise Service. The service will begin at 6:30 A.M. in the City Park.

Come prepared to worship and to enter into the musical part of the service. Please help us by inviting anyone you meet this week.

★   ★   ★

We would like you to make our day complete by coming by our home at _____ next Sunday afternoon.

We hope to have friends and family gathered about us to make the celebration of our Golden Wedding Day a happy one.

★   ★   ★

We would like to see your warm smile and cheerful face in our services next Sunday. We have missed you lately and find there is no one who can quite fill your place. Please make us happy and our services more complete by being in your accustomed place next Sunday.

★   ★   ★

Come help us light more lights in our huge world as we listen to our returned missionary Mr. _____. Be sure to come prepared to make a mission offering. We cannot go to the mission fields but we can help send those who feel called to spend their life in such a dedicated service.

★   ★   ★

I wish I might, I wish I may have the wish
I wish today,
I wish you would attend the service
Held in honor of _____.
Be there early and we will stay late

Just having fun and honoring one
We are all proud of.

★   ★   ★

Be sure to attend a roundtable discussion next Sunday evening. We are all friends but we have different views. We would like to hear your views on the subject of _____.

★   ★   ★

We'll C-E-L-E-B-R-A-T-E !
An ANNIVERSARY —
In our church next Sunday.

★   ★   ★

Join us on Saturday night for a big event !

★   ★   ★

You would feel hurt if you were not invited. We will feel hurt if you do not come, next Friday at _____.

We will celebrate the _____ of our Pastor and his family.

★   ★   ★

Wouldn't you like to be home again? Wouldn't you like to worship once more in the church of your youth?

Come, with a basket lunch, on homecoming day.

★   ★   ★

I know you are getting more invitations to speak than you can possibly accept. Our church wishes so much to hear your message. Will you write and let me know a date you might be able to come and spend an evening with us.

Announcements

We are anxiously looking forward to our Bible Conference. We want this to be a time of real spiritual feasting. Plan to attend and rejoice in the great messages. You will enjoy blessings as you hear Bible scholars, scientist, teachers, bring messages on our modern times and their relation to the Bible.

★ ★ ★

Do you sometimes wish you knew just where to find a certain Scripture? Do you often wish you could explain a passage better? Attend the Bible Conference and learn more about the Bible we believe and love.

★ ★ ★

Plan now to attend our Retreat next month. Beds and meals will be available but you must turn in a reservation.

★ ★ ★

We are looking toward _____ people in Sunday School on Victory Sunday. This is not impossible; it is not even improbable — we can reach this goal. We must set our minds and hearts to accomplish the task.

Dr. _____, teacher in _____ school will lead in a discussion on understanding our modern children. Be sure to attend and get a better knowledge of our children today.

★ ★ ★

Not yesterday, nor tomorrow, nor next week, but tonight in this auditorium we will have the opportunity of a lifetime. A great man and a great speaker will bring us a message on the conditions of the world today.

★ ★ ★

Bold, imposing, majestic is the group of distinguished speakers who will make up the program for the convention.

Much preliminary planning has gone into this carefully-designed program. Attend this meeting, it is your chance to meet men of prominence. Someone, a long time ago advised, "Rub shoulders with all the great men you can. Some of their greatness might rub off on you."

★   ★   ★

If you are a pastor, minister of education, or any type of full time denominational worker, make plans now to attend a retreat in _____ camp. You will grow spiritually, mentally, and socially if you attend this meeting.

★   ★   ★

Next _____ we will as a church observe the Lord's Supper. Come prepared to worship by making a new commitment of your life to service for Christ. The pastor will preach a short sermon on the significance of the Ordinance.

★   ★   ★

Tremendous feats have been accomplished by those who met to pray and left to visit in the name of the Lord. Come to visitation _____.

★   ★   ★

Do we want power in our church? What power in prayer we would have if we all attended the mid-week prayer service.

★   ★   ★

For a deeper insight into the Word attend Prayer Meeting.

★   ★   ★

Don't allow the sunshine and daylight saving time to keep you from filling your spiritual needs. Be in services all day Sunday.

★   ★   ★

We are furnishing a Church Cabin at _____ camp. This will be a "home away from home" for our members this summer. Help us furnish this building with some of your extra furniture.

★   ★   ★

Don't forget the back yard fellowship next Friday evening.

★　　★　　★

We all have many important dates we want to remember; but too often we forget and make other plans. Something very important in our church is the Youth Revival. _____ parents please plan to cooperate by keeping your youth in town that weekend.

★　　★　　★

Don't forget the _____ meeting. A missionary from _____ will be the featured speaker. He is one of our outstanding missionaries. You will be sorry if you fail to hear his message.

The Offering

We are praising the Lord for some increase in our general offerings. We are grateful to all who made a special offering for Missions this month.

★   ★   ★

As we begin a new year we feel encouraged by the approval of an increased budget. Our church will reach out to broader fields this year. We thank the Lord for all who saw fit to enlarge their pledges.

★   ★   ★

A big silver dollar and a little
    brown cent,
Rolling along together they went,
Rolling along the smooth sidewalk.
    When the dollar remarked — for
    the dollar can talk;
You poor little cent, you cheap
    little mite,
    I'm bigger and more than twice
    as bright;
I'm worth more than you a hundred-fold,
    And written on me in letters bold
Is the motto drawn from the pious creed,
    "In God we trust," which all can read.
Yes, I know, said the cent, I'm a cheap
    little mite,
    And I know I'm not big, nor good,
    nor bright.
And yet, said the cent, with a meek
    little sigh,

You don't go to church as often as I.
— Unknown

★   ★   ★

Everything in this world belongs to God. Yet He has promised that if man will seek first the Kingdom of God and His glory other things will be given to him.

★   ★   ★

Give best to God,
Who gave His best;
Give first your heart —
Your nobler part:
    It is your due.

Give all you are,
Give all you have;
Hold nothing back
Lest there be lack
    For God and you.
— Robinson

★   ★   ★

A dollar is as big as the man who possesses it.

★   ★   ★

Again it is our opportunity to focus the attention of our church upon missions. Plan now to make a sacrificial mission offering. Plan now to attend all the special mission programs.

★   ★   ★

Just a reminder that today is our Building Fund Day. Make your offering a little larger than usual.

★   ★   ★

Thoreau, the philosopher wrote long ago, "In the long run, men hit only what they aim at. Therefore they had better aim at something high."

We have aimed at a fine new church building. I believe we will be able to reach our goal.

We are justifiably proud of the accomplishments made in the past year. Now it is time to take stock and look for the new things in the future.

★　★　★

The Offering

Let us bring our tithe into the storehouse.

Let us all be faithful to return a portion of God's bounty to Him.

The granary is dry. We have had lots of extra expense this week. Make your gift a little more today.

Let us get to the business of underwriting the budget of our church.

Reliable estimates show that the cost of living has risen several per cent. If you do not enlarge your pledge over last year you will be giving less.

What is your potential for giving?

★　★　★

Our deepest gratitude to those who made an extra offering last Sunday. All our bills are paid and we start a new church year even, financially.

★　★　★

Get out your check books and let's pay off this note today.

★　★　★

I believe in baptising a man's wallet as well as his heart and life.

★　★　★

"Ye are not your own; for ye were bought with a price."
— I Corinthians 6:19

Have you met any payments on that price?

★　★　★

We can do more than we've ever done
And not be a wit the worse.
For loving never hurt anyone

And giving never emptied a purse.
— Unknown

★   ★   ★

"Upon the first day of the week let everyone of you lay by him in store as God hath prospered him." — I Corinthians 16:2

Now we can get by without money if each member will open his home one day a month for some type of church activity.

Of course, you will have to have things extra clean the day the nursery children meet in your home. Be sure to have plenty of orange juice and cookies, they get hungry before services are over. Don't complain if some parents are an hour late coming after the children. Just change their diapers and wait.

Then the teen-agers may need to meet in your home and garden at least twice a month. They do not intend to break up the furniture. They are just like half-grown colts and they do not intend to break things. Just remember you complained about having to keep up the church. So we did away with church buildings and just pass around the meetings now.

You must take turns preaching and singing because we will not have money to pay the pastor and song director.

What a glorious time we will have. It will not cost a cent, at least not on the Sundays we meet in the other fellow's home.

Oh, by the way you ought to join a few clubs. The church will no longer have money to help out when a family has a tragedy.

★   ★   ★

Lives of skinflints should remind us
We can hoard our dough and when

We check out we'll leave behind us
Kith and kin who'll blow it in.

— Olin Miller

★　★　★

Remember!
That what you possess
In the world
Will be found
At the day of your death
To belong
To someone else;
But what you are,
The time you give,
The service you render,
The tithe and offering
You bring to God
Will be yours
Forever.

— Unknown

★　★　★

Ill fares the land, to hastening ills
　　a prey,
Where wealth accumulates, and men
　　decay.

— Oliver Goldsmith

★　★　★

Some folks just want to make an offering once in awhile.
It reminds me of the henpecked husband.

"Haven't I always given you my salary check at the first
of every month?" he asked his wife.

"Yes, but you never told me you got paid on the first and
the fifteenth, you embezzler."

Our expenses at church go on all month.

★　★　★

An over-spent young man said, "The motor in my car won't start and the payments won't stop." Just like church expenses.

. . . Prayers

We would invest today in the cause of Christ. Help us to invest freely and joyfully.

Help us to invest not only money but life and talents for Thy service.

★ ★ ★

We bring our gifts today with great joy and thanksgiving. May they be gifts of material goods and gifts of good works.

★ ★ ★

Father we know all things come from Thee. Give us the spirit to return a portion into Thy storehouse.

★ ★ ★

Bless the use of these offerings. Bless the ones who bring the offerings and may they return unto them in a cup pressed down and running over with joy.

★ ★ ★

We are glad today to be able to share with those in need. Thank you for all the blessings we have enjoyed this past year as a congregation. Help us in the words of the hymn to say:

> Were the whole realm of nature mine,
> That were a present far too small:
> Love so amazing, so divine,
> Demands my soul, my life, my all.

Bits of Verse and Spice
for Special Days

Lord's Supper

Never in a costly palace did I rest on golden bed.
Never in a hermit's cavern have I eaten idle bread.
Born within a lowly stable, where the cattle round
  me stood,
Trained a carpenter in Nazareth, I have toiled and
  found it good.
They who tread the path of labor, follow where my
  feet have trod;
They who work without complaining do the holy will
  of God.
Where the many toil together, there am I among my own;
Where the tired workman sleepeth, there am I with
  him alone.
I, the peace that passeth knowledge, dwell amid the
  daily strife.
I, the bread of heaven, am broken in the sacrament
  of life.

— Henry Van Dyke

★　★　★

My little cup of faith I bring
To fill at the Eternal Spring;
With many vessels lifted up,
Oh! Jesus, take this little cup.

— Ivan Adair

★　★　★

For the Bride and Groom to Be

To a sweet, brief devotional time,

Add a portion from God's Holy Word,
And then listen together to Him
That the Master's dear voice may be heard.

Speak your thanks for your health and your food
As together you bow for your prayer;
Then together launch out for the day with the Lord
When you've told Him your needs, wants and care.

— J. T. Bolding

★   ★   ★

Never let yourself stay seasick during the voyage of life.

★   ★   ★

We've got to hand it to the girls,
No matter what we say;
If we don't hand it to the girls,
They'll get it anyway.

— S. S. Biddle

★   ★   ★

A groom should remember that the primary function of life is not business. It is the art of living together happily.

★   ★   ★

The kind of woman you decide to marry will determine to a large extent how your life turns out, success or failure.

★   ★   ★

Ladies

A little lass with golden hair,
A little lass with brown,
A little lass with raven locks,
Went tripping into town.

"I like the golden hair the best!"
"And I prefer the brown!"
"And I the black!"
Three sparrows said —
Three sparrows of the town.

"Tu-whit! Tu-whoo!" an old owl cried,
 From the belfry in the town;
"Glad-hearted lassie need not mind
 If locks be gold, black, brown.
Tu-whitt! Tu-whoo! So fast, so fast
 The sands of life run down,
And soon, so soon, three white haired
  Dames
 Will totter thro the town.
Gone then for aye, the raven locks,
 The golden hair, the brown;
And she will fairest be whose face
 Has never worn a frown.
         — Unknown

   ★ ★ ★

Thanksgiving

I don' believe in eating much
 Of Turkey, Pumpkin Pie an' such;
It makes you dream bad dreams at night,
 An' then besides, it's not polite.
So I'm not goin' to stuff and stuff,
 An' act like I can't eat enough.

For me a turkey leg will do,
 With just a slice of breast — or two.
Some liver, gizzard an' a wing.
 An' lots of dressing — that's the thing!
Mashed potatoes, to make me grow,
 Squash and cabbage, they're fine you know.
I must have some cranberries, too,
 An' layer-cake — two pieces will do.
Then of pumpkin pie so yellow —
 One piece, cause I'm a little fellow.
With nuts and apples I shall quit.

An' not ask for another bit.
Tisn't good, the Doctors say
To eat too much Thanksgiving Day.

— Unknown

Christmas

Father calls me William, sister calls me Will,
Mother calls me Willie — but the fellers call me Bill!
Mighty glad I ain't a girl — ruther be a boy
Without them sashes, curls an' things that's
worn by Fauntleroy!
Love to chawnk green apples an' go swimmin'
in the lake —
Hate to take the caster-ile they give for belly-ache!
Most all the time the hull year round there ain't
no flies on me.
But jes' 'fore Christmas I'm as good as I kin be!

Gran'ma says she hopes that when I get to be a man
I'll be a missioner like her oldes' brother Dan.
As was et up by cannib'ls that live in Ceylon's isle,
Where every prospeck pleases an' only man is vile;
But Gran'ma she has never been to see a Wild West show,
Or read the life of Daniel Boone, or else I guess she'd know
That Buffalo Bill an' cowboys is good enough f'r me —
Excep' jes' 'fore Christmas, when I'm as good as I kin be!

Then ol' Sport he hangs around, so sollum like an' still —
His eyes they seem a-sayin'; "What's er matter, little Bill?"
The cat she sneeks down off her perch, a-wonderin'
what's become
Uv them two enemies of hern that used to make things hum!
But I'm so perlite and stick so earnest like to biz,
That mother sez to father; "How improved our Willie is!"
But father, havin' been a boy hisself, suspicions me,
When jes' 'fore Christmas, I'm as good as I kin be!

100

For Christmas, with its lots an' lots uv candies, cakes
   and toys,
Wuz, made, they say, f'r proper kids, and not f'r naughty
   boys!
So wash your face and brush your hair, an' mind yer
   p's and q's,
An' don't bust out yer pantaloons, an' don't wear out
   your shoes;
Say yessum to the ladies, an' yessir to the men,
An' when they's company don't pass yer plate f'r pie again;
But, thinkin' uv the things you'd like to see upon that tree,
Jes' 'fore Christmas be as good as you kin be!

                                — Eugene Field

★ ★ ★

Easter

       The Christ comes forth this blessed day
         And loud the angels sing;
       The barrier stone has rolled away,
         To reign, a deathless king.
       For shall we not believe He lives
         Through such awakening?
       Behold, how God each April gives
         The miracle of Spring.

                          — Edwin L. Sabin

★ ★ ★

Memorial Day

       Over the new-turned sod
         The sons of our fathers stand,
       And the fierce old fight
       Slips out of sight
         In the clasp of a brothers hand.

                    — Albert Bigelow Paine

★ ★ ★

Opportunity

       So here hath been dawning

Another blue day;
Think, wilt thou let it
  Slip useless away?

Out of Eternity
  This new day is born;
Into Eternity
  At night will return.

Behold it afore time,
  No eye ever did;
So soon it forever
  From all eyes is hid.

Here hath been dawning
  Another blue day;
Think, wilt thou let it
  Slip useless away?
                — Thomas Carlyle

★   ★   ★

Somebody said that it couldn't be done,
  But he with a chuckle replied
That "maybe it couldn't," but he would be one
  Who wouldn't say so till he'd tried,
So he buckled right in with the trace of a grin
  On his face. If he worried he hid it,
He started to sing as he tackled the thing
  That couldn't be done, and he did it.
                — Edgar A. Guest

★   ★   ★

Do not then stand idly waiting
  For some greater work to do;
Fortune is a lazy goddess,
  She will never come to you.
Go and toil in any vineyard,

Do not fear to do or dare;
If you want a field of labor,
You can find it anywhere.
— Ellen Gates

★　★　★

Words

I love the sound of kindly words —
I try to make them sing,
And hope I never send one out
To be a hurtful thing.
— Unknown

★　★　★

When I was little
Thought I was big;
Now I'm a giant,
Don't care a fig.

When I was nobody,
Felt quite a chap;
Now that I'm somebody,
Don't care a snap.
— Unknown

★　★　★

What you can do, or dream you can, begin it.
Boldness has genius, power and magic in it.
— Goethe

★　★　★

Your friendship through the years,
Has been a precious thing to me,
A golden chain that time has forged,
With each link a memory.

To hold us close together though
Our paths be near or far

For we shall be friends always
In our home beyond the stars.

— Unknown

★   ★   ★

Today is the day you have to enjoy.
So treasure its blessings.

★   ★   ★

If a task is once begun
Never leave it till it's done
Be the labor great or small,
Do it well or not at all.

— Unknown

★   ★   ★

Silly Susan Scuppernong
Cried so hard and cried so long
People asked her what was wrong.
She replied, "I do not know
Any reason for my woe —
I just feel like feeling so."

— Arthur Macy

★   ★   ★

Words

Keep them back if they're cold or
   cruel,
Under the bar and lock and seal.
The wounds they make, young people,
   Are always slow to heal.

God guard your lips, and ever,
From the time of your early youth,
May the words you daily utter
   Be words of beautiful truth.

— Unknown

★   ★   ★

Sure, this world is full of trouble —
  I ain't said it ain't.
Lord, I've had enough and double
  Reason for complaint;
Rain and storm have come to fret me,
  Skies are often gray;
Thorns and brambles have beset me
  On the road — but say,
    Ain't it fine today?

— Malloch

★   ★   ★

Reach as far as you can and God will reach down the rest
of the way.

Thank You Notes

It was so very thoughtful and kind of you to send the helpful, consoling message during the time of our recent bereavement.

How it does strengthen our hearts to know that others are concerned and that they too understand. We are grateful to you.

★　　★　　★

Heartfelt thanks for your lovely expression of comfort just when my need was so great. What an inspiration you have been to me.

★　　★　　★

How lovely you were to give me such a nice party. The party was so much fun. I will long have memories of the happy time spent in your home.

★　　★　　★

It was a joy and privilege to be in your good home during the revival meeting. Thank you for your gracious hospitality to us and the members of our revival team. The fellowship in your home was a great inspiration to us.

★　　★　　★

I appreciate the work you have done in our Association this year. I am happy that we can have your stabilizing influence in our Association.

★　　★　　★

Thank you for the gift. It came on a day when it was needed! We value your friendship.

★　　★　　★

May I take this opportunity to express my personal gratitude for your very kind and helpful assistance during the time of our recent sorrow.

Your words of comfort and your very personal attention to the family during our time of need was indeed appreciated.

★ ★ ★

Thank you for your time and dedicated effort spent as a committee member this past year.

★ ★ ★

Thank you for the book. I love and treasure books. This one is especially nice both because of its message and because you gave it to me. Give my regards to your wonderful family.

★ ★ ★

Thank you for your cheerful visits, your prayers, and your encouragement. We always appreciate friends in Christ.

Just want you to know we appreciate you more than you will ever know.

★ ★ ★

May the Lord bless and keep you and your loved ones.

★ ★ ★

We cannot put into words the love and friendship we feel in our hearts for you. You have the ability to be warm and sweet to everyone. We love you for just that.

★ ★ ★

Thank you for the refreshing attitude shown at our last meeting. I feel blessed to have warm friends like you.

★ ★ ★

Thank you for the kind resolution of confidence you good men passed unanimously at your last meeting. Thank you for this kindness which means more to me than words can express.

★ ★ ★

Thank you for the privilege and opportunity of spending a week in your church. The services were a great source of spiritual inspiration to me.

★ ★ ★

How is it possible to thank you for all you have done for my family and me. I am grateful the Lord gave me a friend like you.

★ ★ ★

You will always hold a special place in my heart. Your many kindnesses will be one of my most treasured memories.

★ ★ ★

I want you to know how much I appreciated your visit while I was in the hospital. It was such a comfort.

★ ★ ★

Thank you for being such a dear friend. You have a habit of being there just when we need you most.

★ ★ ★

You have brought me special happiness and sunshine with your lovely gift.

★ ★ ★

Whatever else is lost among the years I hope to keep the happy memories of Graduation. Your gift helped make this a very happy time. Thank you for being so thoughtful.

★ ★ ★

Thank you so much for the delicious candy. It made our Christmas much sweeter. We send our love and appreciation to a very lovable couple.

★ ★ ★

How can I thank you enough for the beautiful gift. I appreciate it so much and really needed it. Thank you for the fine example of Christian living you have been to me during my growing up years.

★ ★ ★

My family and I would like to gratefully acknowledge and thank you for your kind expression of love and sympathy.

★ ★ ★

"A word spoken in due season, how good is it." — Proverbs 15:23

My wish for you is that the joy you have brought to our class as a teacher may be returned to you.

★   ★   ★

Thank you for being such a wonderful dad. You are so loved by all your children because you have such an understanding way. We feel we have the greatest dad of all. We wish to give you a vote of thanks for being our dad.

★   ★   ★

I find an ordinary "thank you" entirely inadequate to tell you how much we appreciate your message at our last club meeting.

★   ★   ★

Your graciousness to me during my stay in your home was indeed a great blessing.

★   ★   ★

Dear Friend:

Tonight in a reminicent mood I enumerated some of the many nice things I have been privilged to enjoy these past few years.

What would all the blessings of the past years mean if all the dear friends and loved ones were left out!

So at this season of the year I want to write you and tell you how very much your friendship has inspired and helped me.

Thanks for being my good friend.

★   ★   ★

Dear Friend:

Thank you for the gift. It came when I needed it most. I had been praying and asking God to send someone to cheer me. Thank you for filling a need.

Sincerely,

★   ★   ★

Dear Friend:

I wanted you to know how much your gift, the book

_____, meant to my husband and to me. We read from it almost every day. The words help us bear the great sorrow in our hearts.

Sincerely,

★   ★   ★

To Esther Class:

Thank you for your many expressions of love and thoughtfulness. Our sorrows are much easier, when loved ones are praying and offering their every service the way you did.

With love and appreciation,

★   ★   ★

Dear Mrs. _____:

Thank you for the gift you sent to my shower. You are so sweet and thoughtful to remember me. Words can't begin to express how much gratitude I feel in my heart for such wonderful friends as you and your family. May God bless you is my prayer.

Love,

Congratulations

Congratulations on the publication of your new book. You had something to say and said it in a very forceful way. Your ideas touch our deepest needs in the world at this time.

★   ★   ★

Congratulations on the wonderful message you brought last _____. You certainly showed a depth of conscience and compassion and proved yourself to be committed to a cause.

★   ★   ★

It was a tremendous thrill to see your article in print. I am thankful for people who write with conviction. Hoping to see more of your work.

★   ★   ★

Congratulations to you for winning the prize in the recent contest. You are a very deserving person and our family felt honored to be your good friends.

★   ★   ★

Congratulations on your new position. I feel your employers have chosen well in selecting you. May this be a long and happy experience in your life.

★   ★   ★

You were asked to accomplish a man-sized job and you certainly did it well. Congratulations! We are very proud of the way you handled your assignment as chairman of _____ committee.

★   ★   ★

Congratulations on the lovely musical program you presented to our Club last week. We thoroughly enjoyed it and were so pleased with the talent exhibited there.

★   ★   ★

I have just heard about your beautiful new home. How well you deserve it. I will look forward to the time I can be in your city and have a firsthand look at it. We are so glad you have this new home and know you will make it a place where Christ's love is radiated.

★   ★   ★

At last your new baby has arrived. How wonderful! Life for you will never be the same again. I am so happy for you.

★   ★   ★

Thank you for your invitation to your graduation exercises. I am very pleased to know you were an honor student. We hope life has great things in store for you. The best way to get happiness out of life is to work for it. I know you have worked to graduate and I hope the day is a very happy one.

★   ★   ★

Congratulations on your election to the office of president of our organization.

> May the giver of gifts give this to you,
> A path that leads where the skies are blue,
> A courage to dare and a will to do,
> With a song in your heart and a purpose true
> May the giver of gifts give this to you.
>
> — Unknown

★   ★   ★

I am impressed with your success as a writer. You have already blessed the lives of many people. Congratulations on your new book.

★   ★   ★

As a church we wish to congratulate your committee on the fine work they accomplished this past year. We are deeply grateful for the time and effort spent in our interest.

It gives me great pleasure to say a few words of congratulation to one I esteem so highly. You have worked hard to win the prize. I feel you will go on to other contests and win other prizes. Our whole city is proud of your achievements.

★   ★   ★

Congratulations to the proud and happy parents of a new baby. We know your life will take on a new dimension of happiness. You will have more responsibilities but God gives each new set of parents just the grace and patience they need.

★   ★   ★

Emerson once wrote: The height of the pinnacle is determined by the breadth of the base.

I congratulate you on your success in the teaching field. I feel assured you have reached the top because you studied well and prepared a good foundation.

Letters

... Of Application

Dear Sir:
In accordance with your expressed wishes, I am sending you a copy of my College Transcript.

I would like very much to secure a teaching position in your school. Practice teaching has been my only experience so far. I assure you if you see fit to hire me I will do my utmost to cooperate with the other Faculty members and to follow the policies of the school.

★   ★   ★

Dear Sir:
Due to the fact that my children will be entering college soon I find it necessary to seek employment in your city. I have worked for _____ years in my present position. I would welcome any type of examination of my record as an employee.

My present employer is _____. If you have need of a man of my qualifications, please feel free to write him and ask about my record.

★   ★   ★

Dear Sir:
Mr. _____, who is a mutual friend to both of us, has informed me you are soon to be in need of a new book-keeper.

I have the following qualifications for such a position;

_____.

I would appreciate being considered for this position.

... Of Introduction

Dear Sir:

Mr. _____ spoke to our church recently. I was very much impressed with his message and thought you might like to secure his services for a lecture.

He may be contacted at the following address.

★ ★ ★

Dear Sir:

I would like to call your attention to Mr. _____. He has been a very diligent student in our school and will graduate in May. Since you are personnel manager for your firm I felt you might have an opening for a young man of his training and talents.

★ ★ ★

Dear Sir:

Mr. _____ is a man who is outstanding in any community. He is a community leader and stands for the highest ideals. If you should see fit to consider him for a position in your organization, I feel you will be well pleased with his work. He has a nice family, one you would be proud to introduce to the other members of your group.

★ ★ ★

Dear Sir:

I am writing to recommend one of my brightest young employes. Our organization is small and he has a growing family. He has served us well and loyally. He gets along well with others in the company and we would be glad to keep him. It is at his own request he seeks a larger place.

★ ★ ★

I would like to be there personally to introduce you to Mr. _____. That is not possible, so I want to say just a few words about him. We have been co-workers for a number of years. I have always found him to be most agreeable and willing worker.

He has a nice wife and fine children. They too will fit into any situation agreeably. Call me if you would like further information.

★   ★   ★

Having been a pastor for a number of years I have met many young people. The one who brings you this letter ranks as one of the greatest. He has been dependable and faithful in all the work assigned him. I would be pleased if you see fit to try him on your staff.

★   ★   ★

Mr. _____ has been a reliable student in our school. His grades have been good and his behavior exemplary. He will be missed on our campus for he makes friends easily. I can sincerely recommend him for a position in your organization.

★   ★   ★

Miss _____ is a young lady of high moral standards. She is a Christian first and a very good worker second. You will never have to make excuses for any work she produces.

★   ★   ★

By way of this letter I would like to introduce you to a man who dedicates his time, talents and treasures to the Lord's work. We are sorry to see him move away from our city but feel sure your church and community will improve from his life among you.

★   ★   ★

Let me mention how much I admire Miss _____. She is a well-trained musician. She will add to your church program. She will make a good secretary as well as a music instructor where needed.

★   ★   ★

Though we have never met, I count it a privilege to know

some mutual friends. They have told me of your great work and faithfulness in your community.

I am taking the liberty to write you about a young man who is moving to your community. He is _____. He served our church well and faithfully for all the years he attended college in our city. You will find he performs any task well. He works for the glory of God and not his own glory.

★   ★   ★

I count it an honor to be able to introduce to you, by way of letter, one who has won a place in my respect by his faithful attention to duty. He never asks favors for himself but always tries to be helpful and useful.

. . . Of Recommendation

Dear Sir:

Miss _____ is a fascinating and inspiring young person, The youth in your church will enjoy following her leadership.

She has the qualifications required for a Youth Leader. She graduated from _____ with good records.

★   ★   ★

Dear Sir:

Miss _____ is a young lady who plunges into any task she finds needs doing. She is one of the most alive and lively young people I know.

I would recommend her whole-heartedly for a position on your staff.

★   ★   ★

Dear Sir:

In answer to your questions about Mr. _____ as a public speaker; I have heard him speak to numerous civic and church groups. He is very fine, with a wholesome message. I feel sure you will not be disappointed if you secure his services for a special banquet or meeting.

★   ★   ★

Dear Sir:

I cannot recommend Mr. _____ enough. He is a unique person. He asks first, What may I do to help? Never asks, What will I get out of it?

... Of Resignation

To the Membership of _____ Church:

My Dear Friends:

It is never easy to come to a time of saying goodbye. Friendships grow very dear over a period of years. However, because I feel it is God's will I am accepting a new position offered me.

I have been asked to be a pastor at _____ Church. I have consented to accept the call. I therefore submit my resignation as your pastor, asking that the resignation become effective _____ of this year.

I would like to express a word of gratitude for the cooperation of our splendid Church Staff. I express the love of myself and my family for all the members of the church who have been so gracious and kind to us.

Let us assure you of our continued prayers for your well being and growth.

Most sincerely,

★ ★ ★

Dear Friends:

This has been the most difficult decision I have ever made. The church at _____ has extended me a call and I believe the Lord is leading me to accept it. God's leadership is the most prized possession of a Christian. I have felt that leadership in this decision. Please accept my resignation in the spirit of love in which it is offered.

Respectfully, "In Christ"

. . . Of Condolence

Dear _____:

My heart was made heavy when I received the news of the loss you had sustained. Your dear _____ was truly a child of God. There are so few words one can say at a time of such great sorrow. Rest assured we are praying for God to sustain you at this time.

There will come a great day when you will again be re-united with your precious one. That day will be a time when there will be no more sorrow.

★　★　★

Dear _____ :

Your dear, patient, loving father has gone to be with his own Heavenly Father. What a heritage he leaves to his children! He will long be remembered for the good he has done. He was a strong and noble man. Many friends will grieve with you today.

You have much to be thankful for. God spared his life to a rich and full old age. He died the way he would have chosen. He would never have been happy being an invalid.

We are remembering you in our prayers at this time.

★　★　★

Dear Friend:

The sudden and unexpected death of your loved one has come as a shock to all her friends. What a great loss to all the relatives and friends. We will always remember how sweet and good she was.

★　★　★

I knew your dear son as a happy-hearted boy. He liked to laugh and have fun. He also had a serious side and we often talked of his plans for the future.

123

Please try to believe that God had some greater plans for him or he would not have called him to live in Heaven.

★   ★   ★

May the Master be very near to you during this time of sorrow.

★   ★   ★

We have been taught to believe that nothing on this earth compares with the life beyond and the great eternity. Now with the loss of my friend and your dear loved one, we must cling to our belief in the future life after death.

★   ★   ★

We cannot call the dead back to life, but we can prepare to go to meet them.

★   ★   ★

What has happened in this great tragedy is irrevocable. We must dwell on thoughts of the many happy, pleasant times we have all experienced together.

★   ★   ★

You have lost a precious baby. Your arms feel so empty. My heart bleeds for you in your sorrow. God must have needed a beautiful child for a special place in Heaven's Glory when He called your little one.

★   ★   ★

After death its joys will be
Sweetest pleasures while we live;
'Tis religion must supply
Solid comfort when we die.

After death it's joys will be
Lasting as eternity;
Be the living God my friend,
And my bliss shall never end.
— An old song

★   ★   ★

There is one who is heart-broken,
  And ready for any fate;
His heart has no love token —
  Sad heart that has lost its mate!

He weeps out his heart in the darkness,
  As the song bird sleeps in its nest,
And longs for his absent darling —
  For affection, and peace, and rest.
                                    — Unknown

★   ★   ★

Your loved one has gone through a triumphal archway from earth into the great beyond. He will know no more pain or sorrow. Let us rejoice for his great life past and be glad for his present life in Heaven.

★   ★   ★

I wish to say how much I appreciated the thoughts and prayers of our church during my illness. I also enjoyed and felt lifted up from the visits of the pastor and other staff members. God's blessings on you all.

★   ★   ★

Your thoughtfulness, concern and prayers have been such a blessing. You helped our loved one in her recovery.

In your busy schedule it was sweet for you to take time to express your love and concern.

★   ★   ★

I am grateful for the privilege of having served with you for these past years. My family joins me in expressing our sincerest love and friendship to you.

★   ★   ★

Words are inadequate to express our gratitude for the many deeds performed and gifts given our family during our recent loss and misfortune. We needed help and our

Christian friends supplied it. It is a real pleasure to belong to the fellowship of such wonderful people.

★　★　★

Your prayer at the time of our great loss of our sister was an inspiration and a chord which drew us nearer the source of power. God lifted us up and helped us over the hurdle that we had to take. You are a help to all who call upon you. We are indeed glad you are a part of our church family.

Words from Workers

... An Evangelist

I have been in your community and church only a brief time. It has been long enough for me to enjoy and observe your warm fellowship. I can see with a thrill how dedicated your pastor is, as a result you as a membership seem very dedicated to bringing in God's kingdom. It is a real pleasure to spend this time with you.

★   ★   ★

I am well aware of the plans and preparation which have been made for this crusade. Now we have only a few more days left in which to reap the benefit of your wonderful preparation. Please visit and pray and bring the lost to the services.

★   ★   ★

May I encourage you to press the battle to the gates during the last days of our crusade. You have been so fine to cooperate and pray during these days. The harvest is great we must reap some for the Lord. When the effort is ended we want to rejoice together in the victories.

★   ★   ★

As an evangelist I often grow homesick and many times discouraged. This week you have made me feel at home in your midst. I have felt loved and cared for. Thank you. Please call me any time you are passing through my home town.

... The Musician

I have known so many joys this week in your wonderful church. Thank you for this opportunity of service. The choir and church musicians have gone all out to show me a good time and to cooperate with my plans for the music.

★　　★　　★

I am in full time evangelism. The joy of seeing people find Jesus Christ as Saviour is mine week after week. I have felt a great joy this week in fellowship with such a great church family. The choir has been very faithful to come a few moments early and practice. Each service I have felt the assurance that our music would be fine and good. Thank you for all your many courtesies.

★　　★　　★

Music is vital to any worship service. It is indispensable in an evangelistic crusade. You have indeed lifted your voices in praise and testimony through these services. Your participation in the song services has encouraged me greatly. May I sincerely thank you.

★　　★　　★

Your devotion to good music has inspired me as I worked with you these past years. As I go to a new field I will long remember our good practice periods and our glorious music in the regular services. May God bless and keep each of you is my fervent prayer.

Words of Cheer

Isn't God's love wonderful? You have had sad and terrible trouble, yet you may rest assured He is with you and will bring a brighter day to your life soon.

★　　★　　★

"I am with thee, and will keep thee." — Genesis 28:15

We have God's promise to be with us. I feel so far away from you during this time of your need. Yet in my prayers I have felt closest as I talked to God about your troubles. Only time can heal the deep sorrow. You have much that is good left to live for. Remember the happy times of the past. Nothing can take our memories away.

It is important to give thanks for the blessings of the past and ask for grace to go on in the future.

★　　★　　★

Laugh a little now and then
　It brightens life a lot;
You can see the brighter side
　Just as well as not.
Don't go mournfully around,
　Gloomy and forlorn;
Try to make your fellow men
　Glad that you were born.
　　　　　— Unknown

★　　★　　★

Let your heart find confidence and your mind be serene in the knowledge that God loves you. He will sustain you in this hour of need. You have been a joy and help to many of us in the past. Now rest assured we want to show our love for you.

★　　★　　★

Having you for my friend has made my life seem so worthwhile. Your smile has brightened many of my days. Now you have a weary path of ill health to travel. Have faith in God. He is ruler over disease, over good, and all things beautiful. From my heart I want to assure you we are remembering you in our prayers.

"Aren't the clouds beautiful?" my husband said. We had not had rain for many days and even a small cloud looked welcome.

In my mind I had been composing a letter to you, my dear friend. I wanted to say of your trouble, "Behind every cloud there is a silver lining."

When my husband called my attention to the beauty of the clouds, I realized that there is beauty even in trouble for it draws us closer to our Heavenly Father. It helps us realize how many friends we have. It makes us search for an inner strength to carry on. There is joy and beauty in the clouds that hang over your life now. Good will come from them. Many people will be blessed by your beautiful example of Christian strength and faith. May I just say I love you.

★　　★　　★

The best way to accept sorrow is to follow the example of our Christ and say: "Thy will be done."